Freedom in the Middle East and North Africa

Freedom in the Middle East and North Africa

A *Freedom in the World* Special Edition

Freedom House • New York, NY, and Washington, DC
Rowman & Littlefield Publishers, Inc. •
Lanham, Boulder, New York, Toronto, Oxford

ROWMAN & LITTLEFIELD PUBLISHERS, INC.

Published in the United States of America
by Rowman & Littlefield Publishers, Inc.
A wholly owned subsidiary of The Rowman & Littlefield Publishing Group, Inc.
4501 Forbes Boulevard, Suite 200, Lanham, Maryland 20706
www.rowmanlittlefield.com

P.O. Box 317, Oxford OX2 9RU, United Kingdom

British Library Cataloguing in Publication Information Available

Library of Congress Cataloging-in-Publication Data Available

ISBN 0-7425-3774-9 (cloth : alk. paper)
ISBN 0-7425-3775-7 (pbk. : alk. paper)

Printed in the United States of America

™
The paper used in this publication meets the minimum requirements of American
National Standard for Information Sciences—Permanence of Paper for Printed Library
Materials, ANSI/NISO Z39.48-1992.

CONTENTS

Acknowledgments

Freedom in the Middle East: A Freedom in the World *Special Edition* could not have been completed without the contributions of numerous Freedom House staff and consultants. The Middle East and North Africa country and territory reports were written by Gary Gambill (editor of the *Middle East Intelligence Bulletin* and research associate at the Middle East Forum), Michael Goldfarb (senior press officer at Freedom House), Brian Katulis (senior program officer, RIGHTS program at Freedom House) and Mona Yacoubian (independent consultant specializing in democratization and gender issues in the Middle East and North Africa). Thomas Melia (director of research at the Institute for the Study of Diplomacy and adjunct professor at the Edmund A. Walsh School of Foreign Service at Georgetown University) and Richard Pipes (director of the Middle East Forum) served as regional academic advisors.

Aili Piano, senior researcher, and Arch Puddington, director of research, were the managing editors of the study. Jennifer Windsor, executive director, Adrian Karatnycky, senior scholar and counselor, and Christopher Walker, director of studies, provided overall guidance and support for the project. Amy Phillips and Mark Rosenberg of the New York office supplied critical administrative and research assistance.

Generous financial support for the *Freedom in the World 2004* survey, from which this publication is excerpted, was provided by the Lynde and Harry Bradley Foundation, the Smith Richardson Foundation, the Lilly Endowment, and the F.M. Kirby Foundation.

Freedom in the Middle East and North Africa

Adrian Karatnycky

The questions of democracy and human rights are now central to international discourse about the Middle East and North Africa (ME/NA). This is a consequence of several factors, including greater scrutiny of the political environment that has contributed to the emergence of a deadly global terrorist movement; increased attention to the absence of freedoms by indigenous civic voices and rights groups in the region; and growing international awareness of the Middle East's "democracy deficit."

This democracy deficit, together with major development, education, and women's rights "deficits," has been the subject of the UN Development Program's "Arab Development Report," a study that covers all but two of the countries in this survey and is produced annually by a team of respected Arab scholars.

While some analysts have pointed to Islam as a crucial factor in the region's deficits in democracy and human rights, Freedom House data suggest that Islam is not the reason for the region's poor performance. Indeed, only a small minority of the regimes and governments in the Middle East/North Africa region have transferred significant power to Islamic religious authority. Moreover, our survey data indicate that Islam and democracy co-exist in many diverse settings. Today, approximately half of the world's 1.2 billion Muslims (as defined by tradition and belief) live in electoral democracies where state authority derives from regularly held, generally competitive free and fair elections. Yet, none of the majority-Muslim states in the ME/NA region are democratic. The question is, why is this so?

For over thirty years, Freedom House has produced an annual comparative assessment of the state of freedom throughout the world. The *Freedom in the World* survey examines freedom in two dimensions. The first dimension is political rights: the ability of people to freely and openly elect their government leaders in competitive and regularly contested elections between structures, political parties, and movements representing a broad range of opinion, interests, and policy options. The second dimension is civil liberties: the broad range of personal, associational, cultural, and civic rights essential for the free flow of ideas and the protection of personal autonomy. A series of 25 questions is asked in these two main categories. Countries are then assigned numerical values and evaluated on a comparative basis. Each country is scored on a numerical scale from 1 (representing best practices) to 7 (worst) in the areas of political rights and civil liberties. Countries are also divided into three broader categories: "Free," where rule of law prevails, basic human rights are protected, and there is free political competition; "Partly Free," where some basic political rights and civil liberties exist but are eroded by such factors as rampant corruption, weak rule of law, and religious, ethnic, or other communal strife; and "Not Free," where basic political rights are absent and civil liberties are widely and systematically denied.

A team of nearly forty U.S.-based regional specialists and academic experts takes part in the annual research and ratings exercise. (A more complete explanation of the process can be found in the addenda in this volume, and a more detailed account is available at www.freedomhouse.org.)

The findings in *Freedom in the Middle East and North Africa* are derived from the global volume *Freedom in the World 2004* and encompass events from January 1, 2003 to November 30, 2003.

The volume that follows covers the broad expanse of states from Morocco in Western North Africa to Iran on the Eastern shores of the Arab Gulf. Of the 18 countries, 17 have majority-Muslim populations, and 16 are majority-Arab.

The survey's findings show that among the countries of the Middle East/North Africa, 5 are Partly Free, and 12 are Not Free states, an increase over last year of one Partly Free state (Yemen was rated Not Free in the previous survey and Partly Free this year). Israel is the one country in the region that is rated as Free, meaning its inhabitants possess a broad range of rights respected in the context of the rule of law. Israel also is the region's sole electoral democracy. It is important to note that Israel's rating reflects an assessment of civil liberties and political rights in Israel proper, not the Israeli-Occupied Territories, which are rated separately as "Not Free," given the current significant restrictions placed on Palestinians' abilities to exercise their fundamental rights and liberties.

The Middle East/North Africa region contrasts poorly with the rest of the world in its political rights and civil liberties record. Only one state, or 6 percent of the cohort of ME/NA states, is Free; 28 percent (5 states) are Partly Free; and 66 percent (12 states) are Not Free. By contrast, in the rest of the world, half of the states (87 countries) are Free, 29 percent (50 countries) are Partly Free, and only 21 percent (37 countries) are Not Free.

CHART 1

FREEDOM IN THE MIDDLE EAST AND NORTH AFRICA

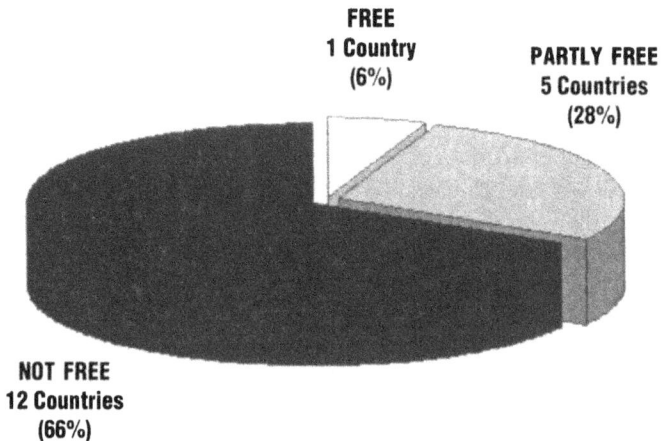

FREE
1 Country
(6%)

PARTLY FREE
5 Countries
(28%)

NOT FREE
12 Countries
(66%)

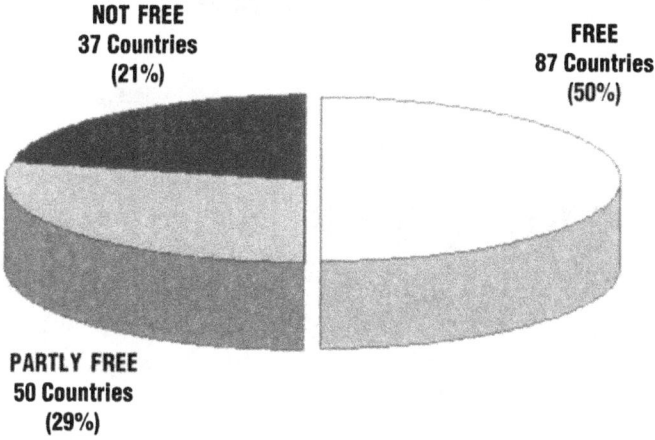

CHART 2

FREEDOM IN THE REST OF THE WORLD

NOT FREE
37 Countries
(21%)

FREE
87 Countries
(50%)

PARTLY FREE
50 Countries
(29%)

The figures in terms of population are even more revealing. Outside the region, 47 percent of the global population lives under freedom. By contrast, in the Middle East/North Africa, only 2 percent (6.7 million people) of the population enjoys a broad range of freedoms. And while only 12 percent of the region's inhabitants (39 million people) live in Partly Free polities, this compares to 21 percent in the rest of the world. Finally, 86 percent (282.3 million people) of the population of the Middle East/North Africa lives under Not Free regimes in which their basic political rights and civil liberties are fundamentally denied. By contrast, 32 percent of the rest of the globe's population lives under similarly repressive and closed societies.

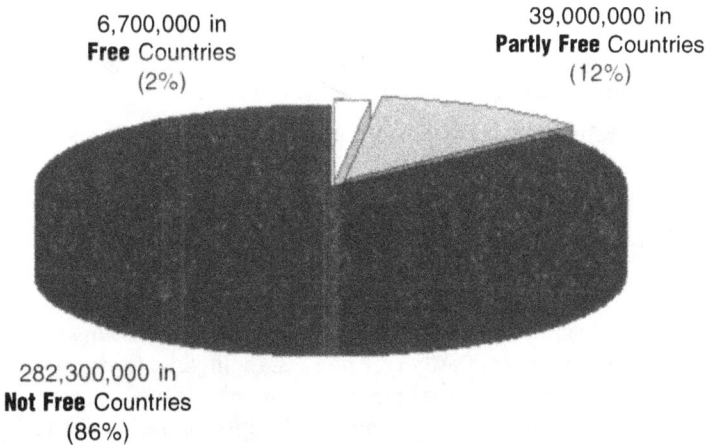

CHART 3

FREEDOM AND POPULATION

Middle East and North Africa

6,700,000 in
Free Countries
(2%)

39,000,000 in
Partly Free Countries
(12%)

282,300,000 in
Not Free Countries
(86%)

CHART 4

FREEDOM AND POPULATION
Rest of the World

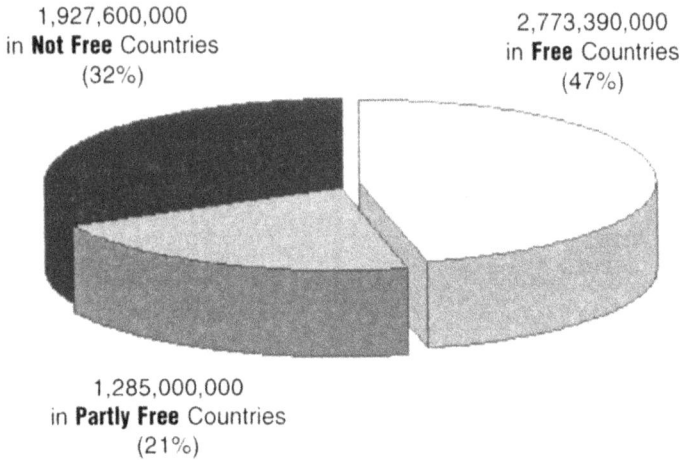

1,927,600,000
in **Not Free** Countries
(32%)

2,773,390,000
in **Free** Countries
(47%)

1,285,000,000
in **Partly Free** Countries
(21%)

Regional discrepancies are equally striking. The Middle East/North Africa region is the least free geographical area in the world. While two-thirds of the ME/NA countries are rated Not Free, there is no other region of the world where the proportion of Not Free countries exceeds 36 percent.

By contrast:

• Even in predominantly poor sub-Saharan Africa, there is significantly more freedom. In Africa, eleven countries are Free, 20 are Partly Free, and 17 are Not Free.

• In the Asia-Pacific region there are 17 Free countries, while Partly Free and Not Free states number 11 and 11, respectively.

• In Western and Central Europe, freedom predominates: 24 of the states in these regions are rated Free. Only Turkey, which is included with these countries, is rated Partly Free.

• In the Americas and the Caribbean there are 23 Free countries, 10 Partly Free, and 2 (Haiti and Cuba) Not Free.

• In Eastern Europe and Central Asia there are today 12 Free countries, 8 are Partly Free, and 7 are Not Free.

Moreover, while approximately 12 percent of Muslims in the Middle East/North Africa live in Free or -Partly Free polities, 73 percent of the Muslims outside the ME/NA region live in Free or Partly Free polities. Eighty-eight percent of Muslims in the ME/NA region live in Not Free states, where their fundamental political and civil liberties are widely and systemically abridged, while less than 27 percent of the nearly one billion Muslims who live outside the ME/NA region live in Not Free countries.

Today, approximately half of the world's 1.2 billion Muslims (as defined by tradition and belief) live in electoral democracies, where state authority derives from regularly held, generally competitive free and fair elections. There are nine majority-Muslim electoral democracies: Albania, Bangladesh, Bosnia, Senegal, Indonesia, Mali, Niger, Nigeria, Sierra Leone, and Turkey. Additionally, large Muslim populations enjoy democratic political rights in such settings as India and Western Europe. All this underscores the fact that there is no inherent incompatibility between Islam and democratic, open political systems.

Yet there are no electoral democracies—not to speak of liberal democratic polities—to be found among the majority-Muslim countries of the Middle East/North Africa. Among the 17 majority Muslim states in the region, eight (Bahrain, Jordan, Kuwait, Morocco, Oman, Qatar, Saudi Arabia, and the United Arab Emirates) are monarchies. Three (Algeria, Egypt, and Tunisia) are states in which there is a dominant ruling party, which uses the state to prevent the emergence of a serious political opposition. One (Libya) is a personalistic dictatorship, and one (Syria) is a under a collective dictatorship of the ruling Ba'athist party. Just three—Yemen, Iran, and Lebanon—have something approaching multiparty political contestation. And of these, only Yemen is clearly moving toward democratic practices. Iran's theocratic council of guardians has taken steps to negate and thwart democratic choice, reversing prior reform momentum, while Lebanon's politics are conducted under the influence of the neighboring Syrian dictatorship. During the period under review, Iraq was under foreign occupation, although the handover of power to indigenous authorities offers an opportunity for the emergence of a system based on political pluralism.

It should come as no surprise that our survey data confirm that, as a cohort, the world's most prosperous states are freer than the world's poorest countries. But the correlations also show that many countries of middling wealth, including a broad array of developing nations, do nearly as well in terms of freedom as high-income countries. Moreover, our research shows that a low level of economic development need not always condemn a society to an absence of freedom.

Low levels of economic development do not appear to be the crucial factor that accounts for the democracy and freedom deficits in the Middle East/North Africa. Only four of the 18 ME/NA countries are among the 91 in the world in which per capita income is below $1,500. Of these poor ME/NA countries, two are Partly Free and two are Not Free. In the rest of the world, 15 of the 87 least developed countries are Free, 37 are Partly Free, and 35 are Not Free.

But the democracy gap and freedom deficit become much more pronounced when ME/NA countries are contrasted to their economic counterparts in middle (average per capita incomes of $1,500-$6,000) and high income (average per capita incomes of over $6,000) countries. Indeed, if we look at the combined cohort of middle and high income countries in the ME/NA region, we find that 1 (7 percent) is Free, 3 (22 percent) are Partly Free, and 10 (71 percent) are Not Free. This weak rights record stands in sharp contrast when compared to the rest of the world's middle and high income countries, where 72 (83 percent) are Free, 13 (15 percent) are Partly Free, and only 2 (2 percent) are Not Free.

TABLE 1

FREEDOM AND GNI/capita

Low-Income Countries (GNI/capita < $1,500)

	Free Countries	Partly Free Countries	Not Free Countries
Middle East/North Africa	0 (0%)	2 (50%)	2 (50%)
Rest of the World	15 (17%)	37 (43%)	35 (40%)

Middle-Income Countries (GNI/capita $1,500-$6,000)

	Free Countries	Partly Free Countries	Not Free Countries
Middle East/North Africa	0 (0%)	1 (14%)	6 (86%)
Rest of the World	35 (76%)	10 (22%)	1 (2%)

High-Income Countries (GNI/capita > $6,000)

	Free Countries	Partly Free Countries	Not Free Countries
Middle East/North Africa	1 (14%)	2 (29%)	4 (57%)
Rest of the World	37 (90%)	3 (7%)	1 (3%)

In addition to ranking significantly lower in terms of political rights and civil liberties than every other international or global cohort to which it is compared, the Middle East/North Africa region has shown little or no progress toward freedom in the last three decades. The rest of the world has seen the number of Free countries more than double, from 42 to 87, over the last 30 years in what scholars refer to as the "Third Wave" of democratization. Yet the number of Free countries in the Middle East/North Africa has declined from two to one, while the number of Not Free states has remained virtually unchanged.

TABLE 2

TRENDS IN FREEDOM

Middle East and North Africa

Year Under Review	Free Countries	Partly Free Countries	Not Free Countries
1973	2 (10.5%)	2 (10.5%)	15 (79%)
1983	1 (6%)	9 (47%)	9 (47%)
1993	1 (5%)	5 (28%)	12 (67%)
2003	1 (5%)	5 (28%)	12 (67%)

TABLE 2, continued

TRENDS IN FREEDOM

Rest of World

Year Under Review	Free Countries	Partly Free Countries	Not Free Countries
1973	42 (32%)	40 (30%)	50 (38%)
1983	52 (35%)	47 (32%)	49 (33%)
1993	71 (41%)	58 (34%)	43 (25%)
2003	87 (50%)	50 (29%)	37 (21%)

Although it is beyond the scope of a brief introductory essay to attempt to explain the wide and longstanding rights and democracy gap in the Middle East/North Africa, it is worth considering some of the leading factors that scholars and political analysts have identified as contributing to the lack of freedom in the region.

Some of these factors are typical of repressive states:

• The concentration of power in the executive and the resulting absence of the separation of powers has led to systems that lack checks and balances, transparency, and adequate oversight of key state institutions.

• In the absence of independent judiciaries and legislatures, the region has seen the emergence of elaborate and intrusive police states that enforce stability in many of these closed societies. Police and state security structures frequently suppress opposition movements and repress free media. At the same time, material rewards are used to co-opt the intelligentsia and therefore limit the emergence of a vibrant civic opposition.

• The absence of a strong rule of law system and legislative oversight does more than erode basic political and civil rights; it also contributes to corruption and cronyism that are detrimental to economic growth and enterprise. In this climate, many countries in the region have failed to develop a vigorous entrepreneurial economy based on innovation.

• Intrusive state mechanisms and statist ideologies that have for decades enjoyed currency in the region have blocked the emergence of competitive economic practices.

• The absence of democratic accountability has in many cases led to the perpetuation of ineffective and corrupt governments.

Other factors that have contributed to the democracy and rights deficits in the ME/NA region are specific to the region's historical development:

• Cultural and legal impediments stand in the way of women's empowerment and equal participation in economic, civic, and political life in the vast majority of countries in the region. The widespread disenfranchisement of women, their relegation to a second class status under the law, and their exclusion from economic life in many ME/NA countries contributes to the region's lack of progress toward fundamental political and economic liberalization. By definition, societies cannot be regarded as free if they deny fundamental and equal rights to half their population.

• Significant oil and gas revenues have bred a syndrome of dependency among indigenous populations and also stifle entrepreneurial initiatives. The income derived from these commodities has conferred vast riches on a small ruling elite that has skillfully used large subventions to their population to buy support, fuel complacency, and increase dependency on the state. A number of recent studies have pointed to the negative correlation between oil and other natural resource wealth and democratic development and sustainable economic systems.

• Monarchy in the Middle East/North Africa has been resistant to reform for most of the last three decades. Many of the region's monarchies have been able to ease pressure for reform by deploying revenues generated from oil, and some in the Gulf States have entered into compacts with religiously conservative movements in a bid to preserve power.

• Politically extremist movements and ideologies—including revolutionary Islamist movements, Salafism, and Saudi-based Wahhabism, which reject tolerance and preach an extreme version of Islam—have enjoyed enduring influence in the Middle East/North Africa.

• For decades, the now-dismantled Soviet bloc exerted sway over the region by educating and training secular elites who in turn contributed to the spread of Ba'athism and pan-Arab socialism.

• A wide variety of authoritarian and totalitarian ideologies in the ME/NA region promote anti-democratic values. At the same time, authoritarian leaders use the existence of extremist groups as a justification for suppressing peaceful democratic dissent and as an excuse for not moving toward free and fair elections.

• Western policies and attitudes towards the region have not enabled political reform and the establishment of accountable institutions. The legacy of past colonial and foreign domination helped create states that lacked significant legitimacy. More recently, Western policy was shaped by U.S. and European alliances with some of the region's worst tyrants. For years, Europe and the United States dealt mainly with regimes and turned a blind eye to the calls for human rights and democracy that issued from courageous independent intellectuals, civic groups, and media in the region. Democracy goals in U.S. foreign policy largely bypassed the countries of the Middle East and North Africa until the events of 9/11. While there is now renewed U.S. and Western commitment to promoting political and economic reform in the region, the populations in the Middle East/North Africa remain skeptical about the seriousness and motives of Western pro-democracy initiatives.

• The failure by the United States, Europe, and the international community as a whole to help resolve the Arab-Israeli conflict reduces the influence of the democratic world on politics in the region and strengthens the hand of anti-Western and anti-democratic movements. A case can be made that the ongoing Israeli-Palestinian conflict is cynically exploited by some of the region's authoritarian rulers in an effort to divert attention from urgent domestic reform issues.

Despite this litany of explanations for the failure of democratic reform to take root in the region, there are some significant signs of ferment and democratic pressure. Polls conducted over the past three years have indicated a strong constituency in the Middle East/North Africa for competitive democratic elections and for governance rooted in civil rights and basic freedoms.

Recent years have brought evidence of significant mass-based ferment in support of democratic reform in Iran, where students and the growing middle class have been at the forefront of pressures for democracy and basic rights.

The removal of Iraq's brutal dictator by a U.S.-led coalition has not resulted in a speedy transition to peace and stability, but at a minimum it has created the possibility for a transition to a system that would be democratically accountable to the Iraqi people.

In Palestine, a healthy infrastructure of civic groups and investigative media have emerged, although their work is impeded both by illiberal Palestinian forces, including Islamist groups and Yasser Arafat's Fatah party, and by the pressures from Israeli occupation.

Yemen's political reform process is gradually moving forward. While the leadership of the country—especially its powerful presidency—has relied on the powers of incumbency to ensure political advantage for the ruling party, a more open media, a more active civil society, and increased national dialogue about democracy are strengthening trends toward greater freedom.

In Jordan, there are signs of modest progress. In 2003, King Abdullah ended rule by decree after more than two years and held reasonably free and transparent, though not fair, parliamentary and municipal elections. In addition, some restrictions on freedom of expression were lifted during the year, and women assumed a higher profile in the government. Nevertheless, it remains to be seen whether King Abdullah's promise of a "new era" of political and civil liberties will come to fruition.

Even in the Gulf states, there are some signs of potential reform momentum. In Bahrain, recent years have seen limited movement toward reform. Voters overwhelmingly approved the National Charter in 2001, thus setting into motion political reforms that led to local elections in May 2002 and national parliamentary elections in October 2002. Leading Shi'a groups and leftists boycotted these elections, protesting restrictions on political campaigning and electoral gerrymandering aimed at diminishing the power of the Shi'a majority. Sunni Muslim groups ended up winning most of the seats in the new National Assembly. Nevertheless, despite this boycott, opposition groups fared well at the polls, and the new cabinet included opposition leaders.

In Kuwait, the 2003 legislative elections did not meet minimal international standards and were tainted by the exclusion of women from voting and by allegations of widespread government-subsidized vote buying. Still, the process featured contestation from a range of political movements, from conservative Islamist to liberal reformist.

Qatar has made very modest progress toward elected legislatures through political reform that included municipal elections and a national referendum on a new constitution in April 2003. The municipal vote resulted in the first election of a woman to public office, and nearly 97 percent of the voters in the referendum approved the new constitution, which creates a very limited—partly appointed and partly elected—legislature.

While most reform initiatives in the Gulf have been launched top-down and in the absence of mass public mobilization, it is increasingly difficult for the Gulf monarchs to ignore public desire for greater transparency and accountability. Although some analysts see recent reforms in the Gulf monarchies as an effort to relieve reform pressure by mimicking democratic practices, others believe steps toward electoral contestation represent movement toward more far-reaching liberalization and pluralism over the long term.

Even in tightly controlled Saudi Arabia, there are modest signs of public activism in favor of greater rights. Groups of citizens have organized a series of petitions calling for democratic elections. While government leaders have met with some of the reform movement's leaders, several peaceful public protests have been broken up and their organizers detained.

As the contents of this volume and the findings of Freedom House's research suggest, basic political rights and civil liberties are widely and systematically denied in most of the ME/NA region. However, there are growing indications of internal civic and public pressure for political reform. Despite the wishes of some of the region's leaders, discussion of the widespread absence of freedom in the Middle East/North Africa can no longer be suppressed, at home or in the international arena. In this sense, the wishes of many of the region's rulers notwithstanding, the impact of democracy and democratic values is perhaps beginning to be felt. Time will tell whether the openings for reform that have emerged will transcend into genuine transition processes towards democracy.

Adrian Karatnycky is Counselor and Senior Scholar at Freedom House.

Table 3

TABLE OF MIDDLE EAST AND NORTH AFRICA COUNTRIES

TREND ARROW	COUNTRY	PR	CL	FREEDOM RATING
	Algeria	6	5	Not Free
	Bahrain	5	5	Partly Free
	Egypt	6	6	Not Free
	Iran	6	6	Not Free
	Iraq	7	5▲	Not Free
	Israel	1	3	Free
	Jordan	5▲	5	Partly Free
	Kuwait	4	5	Partly Free
	Lebanon	6	5	Not Free
	Libya	7	7	Not Free
	Morocco	5	5	Partly Free
	Oman	6	5	Not Free
⬆	Qatar	6	6	Not Free
	Saudi Arabia	7	7	Not Free
	Syria	7	7	Not Free
	Tunisia	6	5	Not Free
	United Arab Emirates	6	6▼	Not Free
	Yemen	5▲	5	Partly Free

PR and CL stand for Political Rights and Civil Liberties

1 represents the most free and 7 the least free rating

▲▼ up or down indicates a modest trend in freedom

⬆⬇ up or down indicates a change in Political Rights or Civil Liberties since the last survey

The freedom ratings reflect an overall judgment based on survey results. See the essay on survey methodology for more details.

NOTE: The ratings in this table reflect global events from January 1, 2003, through November 30, 2003.

Algeria

Population: 31,700,000 **Political Rights:** 6
GNI/capita: $1,650 **Civil Liberties:** 5
Life Expectancy: 70 **Status:** Not Free
Religious Groups: Sunni Muslim (99 percent), Christian
and Jewish (1 percent)
Ethnic Groups: Arab-Berber (99 percent), other (1 percent)
Capital: Algiers

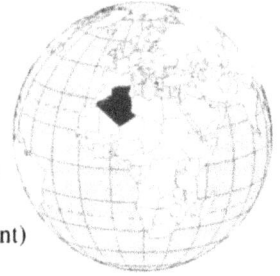

Ten-Year Ratings Timeline (Political Rights, Civil Liberties, Status)

1994	1995	1996	1997	1998	1999	2000	2001	2002	2003
7,7NF	6,6NF	6,6NF	6,6NF	6,5NF	6,5NF	6,5NF	6,5NF	6,5NF	6,5NF

Overview: Violence in Algeria continued to diminish in 2003, yet the root causes of the 11-year conflict remain. The government's lackluster response to a massive earthquake reinforced staunch popular disaffection with the government that derives from long-standing socioeconomic ills and a lack of public accountability and transparency. Mounting political disarray, stirred by upcoming presidential elections, further clouded the scene. However, the government has made some important steps in the human rights arena.

Algeria gained independence in 1962 following 132 years of French colonial rule that ended with a bloody eight-year revolution. Algeria's current conflict can be traced to the 1986 oil market collapse. As oil prices dropped precipitously, Algeria saw its key source of foreign exchange dwindle. Unemployment, housing shortages, and other social ills fed growing popular resentment. The government embarked on a series of quick-fix economic reforms, but neglected to address the deep political roots of the crisis. With no political outlet, Algeria's young men took to the streets in violent riots during October 1988.

Once peace was restored, President Chadli Bendjedid vowed to open Algeria's political system by amending the constitution and legalizing political parties after more than 30 years of single-party rule. Most significantly, the amended constitution paved the way for the government's controversial 1989 decision to legalize the Islamic Salvation Front (FIS), an umbrella organization of Islamist opposition groups with significant grassroots support. In January 1992, the FIS was poised to win a commanding parliamentary majority when the army stepped in, forced President Bendjedid to resign, and cancelled the vote. The FIS was subsequently banned and its leaders imprisoned. The country was placed under a state of emergency that remains in effect.

Algeria's abortive experiment with democracy quickly deteriorated into violence as Islamist militants took up arms against the regime. The loosely structured coalition undergirding the FIS splintered into rival armed factions. As these groups surged at the expense of political moderates, Algeria's Islamist movement turned increasingly radical. A guerrilla-style insurgency erupted in the countryside, while urban-based extremists resorted to terrorist tactics. The resulting bloodletting has left an estimated 150,000 dead. Hundreds of civilians were killed in a series of massacres perpetrated by Islamic extremists. Meanwhile, government-backed militias are believed to have committed mass killings, and human rights groups have accused the Algerian security forces of being responsible for thousands of "disappearances."

In 1997, the Islamic Salvation Army (AIS), the least radical of the armed groups, announced a unilateral ceasefire. While AIS combatants agreed to lay down their arms, extremist offshoots such as the Armed Islamic Group (GIA) and the Salafist Group for Preaching and Combat (GSPC) continued to conduct terrorist attacks on both civilian and government targets.

The 1999 presidential election was severely flawed. Citing government fraud and manipulation, the entire slate of opposition candidates withdrew from the election at the eleventh hour, leaving Abdelaziz Bouteflika to run unopposed. After Bouteflika took office, the government introduced a "civil harmony" law that granted amnesty or leniency to Islamist rebels who renounced violence. According to government sources, some 5,500 members of the armed groups surrendered between July 1999 and January 2000. The GIA and the GSPC continue to wage attacks, with more than 1,100 civilians killed in 2002 and 2,000 people killed in 2001.

Ongoing violence, while diminishing, continued to plague Algeria in 2003. Some estimates maintain that at least 100 people are killed each month by armed groups, security forces, and state-armed militias. In early 2003, the GSPC kidnapped 32 European Sahara trekkers. All were eventually released, although one died in captivity. Although foreigners had been targeted in the violence during the early 1990s, this incident stands as the first such attack in some years. Algerian security forces also continue to mount operations against suspected militant strongholds.

A massive earthquake in May left 2,200 dead and thousands homeless. As with previous natural disasters, the government's inability to respond effectively drew significant popular criticism. Government officials were visibly absent, while Islamic charitable networks mobilized quickly to provide assistance. Some angry residents threw stones at President Bouteflika when he came out to survey the damage. The government established a commission of inquiry into the faulty construction of the scores of apartment buildings that collapsed in the earthquake. Yet, for the majority of Algerians, the tragedy confirmed their perceptions of a government that remains detached and unaccountable to its people. The earthquake's aftermath will contribute to Algeria's festering social ills that include 30 percent unemployment, persistent housing shortages, and a significant proportion of the population living below the poverty level.

A mounting political crisis is overshadowing preparations for the presidential election, currently slated for April 2004. Specifically, a power struggle has erupted between former prime minister Ali Benflis and President Bouteflika. Differences between the two men initially emerged over the question of reform, with Benflis pushing for deeper reforms while Bouteflika opted for a more cautious approach. Tensions between Bouteflika and the National Liberation Front (FLN), their party, escalated after Bouteflika sacked Benflis as prime minister in May. Bouteflika had attempted to short-circuit nomination procedures by securing the FLN candidacy, but was rebuffed. He, in turn, tried to ban the party congress, which proceeded regardless, nominating Benflis as its presidential candidate.

Political turmoil surrounding the upcoming election emanates from an opaque regime in which a relatively small group of military leaders hold the true reins of power.

Sometimes referred to as the *boite noire* (black box), the military decision-making apparatus is the least understood, yet most critical factor in Algerian politics. The generals broker power among themselves through an informal process of consultation and consensus.

Political Rights and Civil Liberties: The right of Algerians to choose their government freely is heavily restricted. Real power in Algeria has always resided with the military. The military leadership's primacy over their civilian counterparts predates Algerian independence, while every leader since Algerian independence has come to power only with the army's blessing. Algeria's civilian president is the nominal head of state, but wields minimal leverage with a small group of generals who retain ultimate authority over political decision making. Parliamentary elections have been largely free of systematic fraud, although the turnout rate in the 2002 elections was the lowest in Algerian history. A Berber electoral boycott coupled with a government ban on the FIS and Wafa parties—two important opposition parties—restricted voter choice, leading to significant apathy.

The press in Algeria is relatively vibrant, although the government often restricts the press either directly through strict defamation laws or indirectly via its control of publishing houses. Journalists have accused the authorities of attempting to silence the media with presidential elections approaching. Several dailies have published searing exposes of government corruption and abuse of power over the last several months, and a number of these papers have met with government harassment. State-run printing houses temporarily stopped printing six dailies on the grounds that the publishing companies were in arrears on outstanding bills. All six papers had published articles implicating high-ranking government officials in various scandals. In one case, the publisher of *Le Matin* was detained at the airport and subjected to legal restrictions following a complaint against him by the Finance Ministry. The paper had recently published an article accusing the interior minister of shady business dealings.

Religious freedom is generally respected. Islam is the state religion, although the government rarely interferes in the practice of non-Muslim faiths. The government monitors closely activities in the mosques, which are closed to the public except during prayer hours.

The government does not restrict academic freedom. During the turmoil of the 1990s, many artists, professors, and intellectuals fled Algeria. However, intellectual life appears to be reawakening. The number of conferences and colloquiums, both international and domestic, is growing, and numerous visas have been granted to international experts in a variety of fields.

Algerian authorities have exploited the state of emergency, in effect since 1992, to curtail sharply freedom of assembly. Citizens and groups are required to obtain government permission prior to holding public meetings. A decree, in effect for the past two years, effectively bans demonstrations in Algiers. In other areas of the country, restrictions on public gatherings are less tight. Emergency laws have also impeded Algerians' rights of association. The government denied registration of certain political parties, nongovernmental organizations, and other associations based on "security considerations."

The 1992 state of emergency laws significantly impinge on due process. While the human rights situation has improved, torture is still prevalent and investigations into human rights abuses are rarely carried out, maintaining a climate of impunity and confusion. The number of political prisoners is estimated to be several thousand, primarily suspected Islamists. Notably, FIS leaders Abassi Madani and Ali Belhadj were released in July at the end of their 12-year sentences.

The initiation of a public debate on human rights issues has been a key positive development. The government has established an ad hoc mechanism to look into the issue of "disappearances," serving as an interface with the thousands of families of the disappeared. The head of a government-established human rights commission has proposed that the Algerian government undertake a number of substantive human rights initiatives. While the degree of independence and freedom to maneuver remain unknown, these developments nevertheless constitute a step in the right direction.

Berbers comprise approximately 20 percent of the population. However, their cultural identity and language are not fully recognized under the law.

Women face discrimination in several areas. The 1984 Family Code, based largely on Islamic law, treats women as minors under the legal guardianship of a husband or male relative, severely restricting their freedoms in several areas.

Bahrain

Population: 700,000
GNI/capita: $11,130
Life Expectancy: 74
Religious Groups: Shi'a Muslim (70 percent), Sunni Muslim (30 percent)
Ethnic Groups: Bahraini (63 percent), Asian (19 percent), other Arab (10 percent), Iranian (8 percent)
Capital: Manama

Political Rights: 5
Civil Liberties: 5
Status: Partly Free

Ten-Year Ratings Timeline (Political Rights, Civil Liberties, Status)

1994	1995	1996	1997	1998	1999	2000	2001	2002	2003
6,6NF	6,6NF	7,6NF	7,6NF	7,6NF	7,6NF	7,6NF	6,5NF	5,5PF	5,5PF

Overview: After taking significant steps to reform its political system in 2001 and 2002, Bahrain pursued the reform process more slowly during 2003, effecting few significant developments on political rights and civil liberties.

The al-Khalifa family, which has ruled Bahrain for more than two centuries, comes from Bahrain's minority Sunni Muslim population in this mostly Shi'a Muslim country. Bahrain gained independence in 1971 after more than a hundred years as a British protectorate. The country's first constitution provided for a national assembly with both elected and appointed members, but the king dissolved the assembly in 1975 because the assembly attempted to end al-Khalifa rule; the al-Khalifa family ruled without the national assembly until 2002.

In 1993, the king established a consultative council of appointed notables, although this advisory body had no legislative power and did not lead to any major policy shifts. In 1994, Bahrain experienced protests and clashes that left more than 40 people dead, thousands arrested, and hundreds either imprisoned or exiled. The unrest was sparked by arrests of prominent individuals who had petitioned for the reestablishment of democratic institutions such as the national assembly.

Sheikh Hamad bin Isa al-Khalifa's accession to the throne following his father's death in 1998 marked a turning point in Bahrain. Hamad released political prisoners, permitted the return of exiles, and did away with emergency laws and courts. He also introduced the National Charter, which set a goal of creating a constitutional monarchy with an elected parliament, separation of powers with an independent judicial branch, and rights guaranteeing women's political participation. In February 2001, voters overwhelmingly approved the National Charter, setting into motion political reforms that led to local elections in May 2002 and national parliamentary elections in October 2002. Leading Shi'a groups and leftists boycotted these elections, protesting restrictions on political campaigning and electoral gerrymandering aimed at diminishing the power of the Shi'a majority. Sunni Muslim groups ended up winning most of the seats in the new National Assembly. Despite this boycott, opposition groups fared well at the polls, and the new cabinet included opposition figures such as Majed Alawi, the former leader of the London-based Bahrain Freedom Movement.

Since taking office in 2002, the new government and National Assembly have not pressed forward with any significant steps to reform Bahrain's political system. In the first few months of 2003, the focus was on regional events, with protestors taking to the streets against the war in Iraq. Bahrain served as the headquarters of the U.S. Navy's Fifth Fleet in the Persian Gulf.

Political Rights and Civil Liberties:

Bahraini citizens do not have the ability to choose the leader with the most power in Bahrain, the king. According to Bahrain's 2002 constitution, the king is the head of all three branches of government. He appoints cabinet ministers and members of the Consultative Council. The National Assembly consists of 40 popularly elected members of the Representative Council and 40 members of the Shura Council appointed by the king. The National Assembly may propose legislation, but the cabinet must draft the laws. Formal political parties are illegal in Bahrain, but the government allows political societies or groupings to operate and organize activities in the country.

Freedom of expression is limited in Bahrain, which received a low 117 ranking in the 2003 press freedom ranking of the media watchdog group Reporters Sans Frontieres. The government owns all broadcast media outlets, but there is a stronger degree of freedom in newspapers, many of which are privately owned. In the fall of 2003, the National Assembly began debating a new press law aimed at expanding press freedoms.

Mansoor al-Jamri, the son of a prominent Shiite dissident living in exile and editor in chief of the independent daily *Al-Wasat*, was brought to court for defying a gag order that sought to prevent press coverage of the March arrest of five men suspected of planning a terrorist attack. Al-Jamri and a journalist for *Al-Wasat*, Hussein Khalaf, were prosecuted for publishing the story of the release of three of the suspects. An estimated one-third of the population has access to the Internet, mostly through the National Telephone Company. Though Internet and e-mail access has generally been unrestricted, there are reports of government monitoring of e-mails.

Islam is the state religion. However, non-Muslim minorities are generally free to practice their religion. According to the law, all religious groups must obtain a permit from the Ministry of Justice and Islamic affairs to operate, although the government has not punished groups that have operated without this permit. Though Shi'a in Bahrain constitute a majority of the citizenry, they are underrepresented in government and face discrimination in the workplace. In 2003, the Bahraini government began debating a proposed unified personal status code that would seek to bridge the Sunni-Shi'a division in legal codes governing family affairs such as marriage, divorce, and inheritance.

The constitution provides for freedom of assembly, and demonstrations and open public discussion are generally permitted. Bahrain has seen strong growth in the number of nongovernmental organizations working in charitable activities, human rights, and women's rights in recent years. Bahrainis have the right to establish independent labor unions without government permission. A royal decree giving workers the right to form labor unions also imposed limits, including a two-week notice to the company before a strike and a prohibition on strikes in vital sectors such as security, civil defense, transportation, hospitals, communications, and basic infrastructure. Labor unions figured prominently on the reform agenda in 2003, with a number of new unions created, including the Bankers' Union. Nearly 200,000 of the 700,000 people living in Bahrain are migrant workers, who are sometimes subjected to mistreatment without legal recourse and protections.

With unemployment among Bahraini citizens estimated at 25 percent, the government began to institute a "Bahrainization" program aimed at replacing foreign workers with Bahraini citizens and extending social protections to the unemployed. Bahrain reportedly plans to cease issuing visas to many migrant workers after 2005, hoping to satisfy the demands of unemployed Bahrainis, many of whom took to the streets in protest against the lack of jobs.

The judiciary is not independent of the executive branch of government. The king appoints all judges, and courts have been subject to government pressure. In September, Bahrain sponsored the Arab Judicial Forum, a conference that brought together government and nongovernmental leaders from the Middle East to discuss judicial independence and reform. The Ministry of the Interior is responsible for public security within the country and oversees the police and internal security services, and members of the royal family hold all security-related offices. The constitution provides rule-of-law protections, and government authorities generally respect these protections. Since the government's abolition of the State Security Act in 2001, the judiciary has refused requests by the police to hold detainees longer than 60 hours

Women are under-represented politically; no woman has been elected to office in municipal or legislative elections. The king appointed six women to the Consultative Council. Women are generally not afforded equal protections under the law. In April, the Women's Petition Committee issued a demand supported by 1,700 people to reform the personal status and family laws, the first petition of this type in Bahrain's history. Leading religious scholars expressed opposition to this proposed reform, and no progress was made on the effort to change the personal status and family laws.

Egypt

Population: 72,100,000   **Political Rights:** 6
GNI/capita: $1,530   **Civil Liberties:** 6
Life Expectancy: 68   **Status:** Not Free
Religious Groups: Muslim [mostly Sunni] (94 percent),
other [including Coptic Christian] (6 percent)
Ethnic Groups: Eastern Hamitic stock [Egyptian, Bedouin,
Berber] (99 percent), other (1 percent)
Capital: Cairo

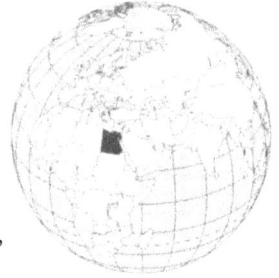

Ten-Year Ratings Timeline (Political Rights, Civil Liberties, Status)

1994	1995	1996	1997	1998	1999	2000	2001	2002	2003
6,6NF	6,6NF	6,6NF	6,6NF	6,6NF	6,6NF	6,5NF	6,5NF	6,6NF	6,6NF

Overview:

In the face of mounting economic problems, the war in Iraq, and American calls for democratization in the Arab world, Egypt witnessed a growing chorus of demands for political change by academics, journalists, and political opposition leaders in 2003. Although the government cracked down on unauthorized demonstrations during the year, it introduced a number of limited reforms and tolerated more open public discussion of the country's political future.

Egypt formally gained independence from Great Britain in 1922 and acquired full sovereignty following the end of World War II. After leading a coup that overthrew the monarchy in 1954, Colonel Gamel Abdel Nasser established a repressive police state, which he ruled until his death in 1970. The constitution adopted in 1971 under his successor, Anwar al-Sadat, established a strong presidential political system with nominal guarantees for most political and civil rights that were not fully respected in practice.

Following the assassination of Sadat in 1981, Hosni Mubarak became president and declared a state of emergency, which he has since renewed every three years (most recently in February 2003). The ruling National Democratic Party (NDP) dominates the tightly controlled political system. In the early 1990s, Islamic fundamentalist groups launched a violent insurgency, prompting the government to jail thousands of suspected dissidents and crack down on political dissent. Although the armed infrastructure of Egyptian Islamist groups had been largely eradicated by 1998, the government continued to restrict political and civil liberties.

High levels of economic growth in the late 1990s temporarily alleviated the underlying socioeconomic problems, particularly poverty and high unemployment among college graduates, that appeared to fuel broader public support for Islamist militancy. However, the country has experienced an economic slowdown over the last three years. Since the September 11, 2001 attacks on the United States, foreign exchange earnings from tourism revenue, oil sales, Suez Canal receipts, and expatriate remittances have declined and foreign direct investment has fallen.

Egypt's economic problems became even more acute in 2003. In late January, the government abandoned its "managed peg" currency regime and adopted a floating exchange rate, causing the pound to depreciate substantially during the course of the year. This devaluation, along with a reduction of subsidies on basic commodities, sparked an estimated 10 to 20 percent increase in the cost of living. In September, the World Bank's country director in Egypt warned that the poverty rate may be increasing for the first time since the mid-1990s.

Economic reforms needed to attract foreign investment have progressed slowly because of fears that austerity measures will undermine political stability. In June, U.S. trade representative Robert Zoellick stated that Egypt had "a long way to go" before it became a serious candidate for a free trade agreement with the United States because of the government's failure to undertake reforms in areas such as intellectual property protection, customs regulations, money laundering, taxation, and privatization. High-profile corruption trials of former government officials and businessmen continued in 2003, but critics allege that the anticorruption campaign has spared leading politicians.

The government's stated position of neutrality in the conflict between Iraq and the U.S.-led coalition exacerbated public anger. In the weeks leading up to the coalition invasion of Iraq in March, small-scale rallies ostensibly organized to protest the war became venues for protesting the government's performance at home. The authorities reacted by deploying riot police to contain illegal demonstrations and arresting dozens of activists suspected of organizing them, while allowing a number of docile, officially sanctioned antiwar rallies. After an estimated 20,000 people gathered in Cairo on the first day of the war to demonstrate against the invasion, thousands of riot police were deployed to prevent a repeat, using water cannons, truncheons, and dogs to disperse demonstrators. Hundreds of people were injured and around 800 were detained, including two members of parliament. Several dozen people arrested during and after the rally were held without charge for weeks.

After the fall of Baghdad, the government initiated a series of limited reforms, such as the abolition of state security courts and hard-labor prison sentences; initiated a wide-ranging dialogue with legal opposition parties; and tolerated more open discussion of previously taboo topics. However, there were few signs that far-reaching political change is on the horizon.

Political Rights and Civil Liberties: Egyptians cannot change their government democratically. As a result of government restrictions on the licensing of political parties, state control over television and radio stations, and systemic irregularities in the electoral process, the 454-seat People's Assembly (Majlis al-Sha'b), or lower house of parliament, is perpetually dominated by the ruling National Democratic Party (NDP), as is the partially elected upper house, the Consultative Council (Majlis al-Shura), which functions only in an advisory capacity. There is no competitive process for the election of the president; the public is entitled only to confirm in a national referendum the candidate nominated by the People's Assembly for a six-year term. The assembly has limited influence on government policy, and the executive initiates almost all legislation. The president directly appoints the prime minister, the cabinet, and the governors of Egypt's 26 provinces.

Political opposition in Egypt remains weak and ineffective. A ban on religious parties prevents the Muslim Brotherhood and other mainstream Islamists from organizing politically, although they typically compete in elections as independents or members of secular parties. Political parties cannot be established without the approval of the Political Parties Committee (PPC), an NDP-controlled body affiliated with the Consultative Council. The PPC has approved the formation of only two new political parties in the last 21 years and routinely rejects applications. Most recently, in November, it denied an application by the Social Constitution Party.

Freedom of the press is limited. The government owns and operates all ground-broadcast television stations. Although three private satellite television stations have been established since 2001, their owners have ties to the government and their programming is subject to state influence. In October, Dream TV, owned by business mogul Ahmed Bahgat, canceled a program on well-known political thinker Muhammad Hassanein Heikal after government officials objected to its content. All radio stations are owned by the government, with the exception of two stations owned by a private company, Nile Radio Production, that were allowed to begin broadcasting in the summer of 2003. However, those two stations received licenses only on the condition that they restrict their programming to entertainment. Egypt's three leading daily newspapers are state controlled, and their editors are appointed by the president. The government encourages legal political parties to publish newspapers and exercises indirect control over them through its monopoly on printing and distribution, but heavily restricts licensing of nonpartisan newspapers. Strictly speaking, only foreign publications are subject to direct government censorship, but most privately owned publications, such as the English-language *Cairo Times*, have been forced to register abroad (usually in Cyprus) and are therefore subject to censorship.

Press freedom is further restricted by vaguely worded statutes in the Press Law, the Publications Law, the penal code, and libel laws. Direct criticism of the president, his family, or the military can result in the imprisonment of journalists and the closure of publications. Discussion of tensions between Muslims and Christians in Egypt and expression of views regarded as anti-Islamic are also proscribed. In June, two journalists convicted of slander in 1998 lost their appeal and began serving one-year prison sentences, but they were released three weeks later pending the outcome of a petition by the press syndicate. Later that month, the weekly newspaper of the Takaful party, *Al-Sadaa*, was suspended, apparently because of its harsh anti-American diatribes, although no reason was given. The government does not significantly restrict or monitor Internet use, but publication of material on the Internet has been prosecuted under the same statutes as regular press offenses. Academic freedom is generally respected in Egypt, though professors have been prosecuted for political and human rights advocacy outside of the classroom.

Islam is the state religion, and the government directly controls most mosques, appoints their preachers and other staff, and closely monitors the content of sermons. It is presently implementing a plan to establish control over thousands of small, unauthorized mosques (known as *zawaya*) located in residential buildings. Most Egyptians are Sunni Muslim, but Coptic Christians constitute less than 6 percent of the population, and there are small numbers of Jews, Shiite Muslims, and Baha'is. Although non-Muslims are generally able to worship freely, the government has seized church-owned property and frequently denies permission to build or repair churches. Muslim extremists have carried out several killings of Coptic villagers in recent years and frequently burn or vandalize Coptic homes, businesses, and churches.

Freedom of assembly and association is heavily restricted. Organizers of public demonstrations, rallies, and protests must receive advance approval from the Ministry of the Interior, which is rarely granted. Hundreds of people who attended illegal demonstrations during the year were arrested and detained by State Security Intelligence (SSI) personnel. A new law regulating nongovernmental organizations (NGOs) went into effect in 2003.The Law of Associations prohibits the establishment of associations "threatening national unity [or] violating public morals," prohibits NGOs from receiving foreign grants without the approval of the Ministry of Social Affairs (which generally blocks funding to human rights defenders and advocates of political reform), requires members of NGO governing boards to be approved by the ministry, and allows the ministry to dissolve NGOs without a judicial order. In June, two existing human rights groups were denied registration under the new law— the New Woman Research Center (NWRC) and the Land Center for Human Rights (LCHR). Although an administrative court subsequently overruled the ministry's decision to reject NWRC's application, it is not yet clear whether the ministry will respect this judgment. Some groups have avoided the new NGO restrictions by registering as law firms or civil companies.

In April 2003, the People's Assembly approved sweeping changes to Egypt's socialist-era labor laws. Under the previous laws, workers were prohibited from striking, but enjoyed virtually absolute job protection—an employee who had held his job for over a year could not be legally terminated unless he committed a "grave" breach of his contract obligations. In practice, however, these laws were not enforced outside of the public sector. Private business owners, with the collusion of government regulators, circumvented the rules by not providing their workers with employment contracts or making them sign undated letters of resignation before being hired. According to one study, 82 percent of the jobs added between 1988 and 1998 in the private, nonagricultural sector in Egypt were not protected by a formal employment contract. The new Unified Labor Law allows employers to lay off workers, with compensation, and lifts the ban on strikes. However, the new law requires that strikes be approved by two-thirds of a union's members and limits the right to strike to "nonstrategic" industries. The government-backed Egyptian Trade Union Federation remains the only legal labor federation.

Egypt's regular judiciary is widely considered the most independent and impartial in the Arab world. The Supreme Judicial Council, a supervisory body of senior judges, nominates and assigns most judges. However, political and security cases are usually placed under the jurisdiction of exceptional courts that are controlled by the executive branch and deny defendants many constitutional protections. The State Security Courts, responsible for trying most defendants charged with political offenses, were abolished in June. However, the government also changed the penal code to grant prosecutors in regular cases most of the extraordinary powers that once resided with these courts. For example, prosecutors now have the authority of investigating judges and can detain individuals for up to six months without charge.

Two exceptional court systems remain in place. The Emergency State Security Courts, empowered to try defendants charged with violating decrees promulgated under the Emergency Law, issues verdicts that cannot be appealed and are subject to ratification by the president. Although judges are usually selected from the civilian judiciary, they are appointed directly by the president. Since 1992, civilians charged with terrorism and other security-related offenses have often been referred by the president to military courts. Since military judges are appointed by the executive branch to short, renewable, two-year terms, these tribunals lack independence. Verdicts by military courts are subject to review only by a body of military judges and the president. Moreover, evidence produced by the prosecution in cases before the military courts often consists of little more than the testimony of security officers and informers. Allegations of forced confessions by defendants are routine.

Although Egyptian officials said in mid-2003 that henceforth only terrorism and other security-related offenses will be tried in emergency courts, this pledge has not been upheld. Ashraf Ibrahim, a vocal opposition activist who helped expose police brutality during the March demonstrations, was arrested in April and detained for four months before being charged in the emergency courts with, among other things, "weakening the prestige of the state by disseminating false information."

The Emergency Law restricts many basic rights. Its provisions allow for the arrest and prolonged detention without charge of suspects deemed a threat to national security. In November 2002, the UN Committee against Torture concluded that there is "widespread evidence of torture and ill-treatment" of suspects by the SSI apparatus. According to local and international human rights organizations, at least three people died in 2003 as a result of suspected torture in police or SSI custody. The Emergency Law also empowers the government to wiretap telephones, intercept mail, and search persons and places without warrants. In mid-2003, parliament passed legislation weakening judicial oversight of wiretaps.

Local and international human rights organizations estimate that more than 10,000 people are currently detained without charge on suspicion of security or political offenses, and that several thousand who have been convicted are serving sentences on such charges. In September, the government released several hundred members of the radical Islamist group Gemaa al-Islamiyya, but scores of other suspected Islamist militants were arrested during the year.

Although the constitution provides for equality of the sexes, some aspects of the law and many traditional practices discriminate against women. Unmarried women under the age of 21 are not permitted to obtain passports without permission from their fathers. Muslim female heirs receive half the amount of a male heir's inheritance (Christians are not subject to provisions of Islamic law governing inheritance matters). Domestic violence is common, and there are no laws against marital rape. Job discrimination is evident even in the civil service. The law provides for equal access to education, but the adult literacy rate of women lags behind that of men (34 and 63 percent, respectively). Female genital mutilation is practiced in Egypt, despite government efforts to eradicate it. In January, the government appointed Egypt's first-ever female judge. In September, the ruling NDP initiated legislation that will allow women who marry foreigners to pass Egyptian citizenship on to their children.

Iran

Population: 66,600,000   **Political Rights:** 6
GNI/capita: $1,680   **Civil Liberties:** 6
Life Expectancy: 69   **Status:** Not Free
Religious Groups: Shi'a Muslim (89 percent),
Sunni Muslim (10 percent), other (1 percent)
Ethnic Groups: Persian (51 percent), Azeri (24 percent),
Gilaki and Mazandarani (8 percent), Kurd (7 percent),
Arab (3 percent), other (7 percent)
Capital: Tehran

Ten-Year Ratings Timeline (Political Rights, Civil Liberties, Status)

1994	1995	1996	1997	1998	1999	2000	2001	2002	2003
6,7NF	6,7NF	6,7NF	6,7NF	6,6NF	6,6NF	6,6NF	6,6NF	6,6NF	6,6NF

Overview:

Efforts by reformist politicians who control the presidency and parliament to further expand social and political freedoms remained stymied in 2003 as a result of opposition from appointive bodies controlled by hardline clerics. The authorities significantly increased restrictions on press freedom and began systematic censoring of Internet content during the year. Thousands of participants in antigovernment protests were detained by security forces, and scores of political activists and journalists were indicted for peaceful activities.

In 1979, Iran witnessed a tumultuous revolution that ousted a hereditary monarchy marked by widespread corruption and brought into power the exiled cleric Ayatollah Ruhollah Khomeini. The constitution drafted by his disciples provided for a president and parliament elected through universal adult suffrage, but unelected institutions controlled by hardline clerics were empowered to approve electoral candidates and certify that the decisions of elected officials are in accord with Sharia (Islamic law). Khomeini was named Supreme Leader and invested with control over the security and intelligence services, armed forces, and judiciary. After his death in 1989, the role of Supreme Leader passed to Ayatollah Ali Khamenei, a middle-ranking cleric who lacked the religious credentials and popularity of his predecessor. The constitution was changed to consolidate his power and give him final authority on all matters of foreign and domestic policy.

Beneath its veneer of religious probity, the Islamic Republic gave rise to a new elite that accumulated wealth through opaque and unaccountable means. By the mid-1990s, dismal economic conditions and a demographic trend toward a younger population had created widespread hostility to clerical rule and a coalition of reformers began to emerge within the ruling elite, advocating a gradual process of political reform, economic liberalization, and normalization with the outside world that was designed to legitimize, not radically alter, the current political system. In 1997, former culture minister Mohammed Khatami was allowed by the ruling clerics to run for president; he won nearly 70 percent of the vote. Khatami's administration made considerable strides over the next few years in expanding public freedoms. More than 200 independent newspapers and magazines representing a diverse array of viewpoints were established during his first year in office, and the authorities relaxed the enforcement of strict Islamic restrictions on social interaction. Reformists won 80 percent of the seats in the country's first nationwide municipal elections in 1999 and took the vast majority of seats in parliamentary elections the following year, gaining the power, for the first time, to legislate major changes in the political system.

The 2000 parliamentary elections prompted a backlash by hardline clerics that continues to this day. More than 100 reformist newspapers have been shut down by the conservative-controlled judiciary during the last three years, and hundreds of liberal journalists, students, and political activists have been jailed. Reform legislation approved by parliament has been repeatedly vetoed by hardliners.

Although Khatami was reelected in 2001 with 78 percent of the vote, he has been unwilling to use this popular mandate to advance the reform process or even to preserve the expansion of civil liberties achieved during his first three years in office. He has refused to call a national referendum to approve legislation that would advance the reform process and continually implores citizens to refrain from demonstrating in public. The most powerful weapon at the president's disposal is the threat of resignation; few observers believe that the "rump" clerical regime that would remain after his departure would be able to maintain control of the country. Although Khatami has repeatedly hinted that he will step down if hardline clerics continue to veto reformist legislation, his failure to act on these threats has made them ineffectual.

Khatami's reluctance to challenge ruling theocrats has led many Iranians to abandon hopes that the political system can be changed from within. The results of a government-conducted poll, published by the Iranian daily *Yas-I No* in June 2003, indicated the depths of this disillusionment: 45 percent of the population would support political change brought about by foreign intervention. Record low turnout for municipal elections in February 2003 showed that the ability of reformist politicians to mobilize the public has deteriorated markedly. In major urban centers, hardline candidates captured most city council seats.

Gridlock between government moderates and hardliners has also obstructed much-needed economic reforms. Although Iran possesses the world's third-largest oil reserves and second-largest natural gas reserves, the government has been unable to generate enough economic growth to reduce the country's soaring unemployment rate. Economic reforms have recently been made in some areas, such as trade liberalization, the establishment of private banks, the approval of a foreign direct investment law, and the amendment of tax laws, but there has been no major restructuring of the economy. According to the IMF, Iran has the highest rate of brain drain in the world, with 160,000 people emigrating to greener pastures last year alone. Among those who remain behind, drug use, clinical depression, and suicide rates among youth are at an all-time high.

In June, Iran witnessed the largest wave of antigovernment demonstrations in four years. The unrest began with a rally by a few hundred students at Tehran University, but appeals by dissident Iranian satellite stations in Los Angeles led thousands of ordinary Iranians to join the protests, which spread to other major Iranian cities. Whereas public demonstrations once exclusively targeted Khamenei and other hardline clerics, calls for Khatami's resignation were prevalent. An estimated 4,000 demonstrators were arrested by the authorities, about half of whom were detained for more than a week, and hundreds were wounded by hardline vigilantes. Khatami's tepid response to the mass arrests led prominent student leaders to publicly withdraw their support for the president. Within the broader reform movement, Khatami and other government "moderates" are increasingly accused not just of being ineffective, but of willingly serving as a democratic façade for an oppressive regime.

Meanwhile, Iran faced new foreign policy challenges in 2003. Although Iranian officials welcomed the American-led ouster of Iraqi President Saddam Hussein in April, reformers and hardliners alike remained suspicious of U.S. promises to establish a representative political system in Baghdad. In June, senior American officials publicly called for a change of government in Tehran. In November, the International Atomic Energy Agency (IAEA) issued a report showing that Iran had been conducting clandestine nuclear research for decades. Although Iran agreed to halt illicit research and allow more intrusive inspections, the IAEA report bolstered U.S. claims that the Islamic Republic has an active nuclear weapons program.

Political Rights and Civil Liberties:

Iranians cannot change their government democratically. The most powerful figure in the Iranian government is the Supreme Leader (Vali-e-Faghih); he is chosen for life by the Assembly of Experts, a clerics-only body whose members are elected to eight-year terms by popular vote from a government-screened list of candidates. The Supreme Leader is commander in chief of the armed forces and appoints the leaders of the judiciary, the heads of state broadcast media, the commander of the Islamic Revolutionary Guard Corps (IRGC), the Expediency Council, and half the members of the Council of Guardians. Although the president and parliament are responsible for designating cabinet ministers, the Supreme Leader exercises de facto control over appointments to the Ministries of Defense, Interior, and Intelligence.

All candidates for election to the presidency and 290-seat unicameral parliament are vetted for strict allegiance to the ruling theocracy and adherence to Islamic principles by the 12-person Council of Guardians, a body of six clergymen appointed by the Supreme Leader and six laymen selected by the head of the judiciary chief (the latter are nominally subject to parliamentary approval). Of the 814 candidates who declared their intention to run in the 2001 presidential election, only 10 were approved.

The Council of Guardians also has the power to reject legislation approved by the parliament (disputes between the two are arbitrated by the Expediency Council, another nonelected conservative-dominated body, currently headed by former president Ali Akbar Rafsanjani). For example, during the year, the Council of Guardians rejected bills that would have eased the ban on satellite dishes, ended its power to screen candidates for elected office, required Iran to adopt UN conventions on eliminating torture and on ending discrimination against women, and allowed jury trials in an open court for journalists.

Freedom of expression is limited. The government directly controls all television and radio broadcasting and succeeded in jamming broadcasts by dissident satellite stations following the June demonstrations (reportedly after receiving assistance from Cuba). The Press Court has extensive procedural and jurisdictional power in prosecuting journalists, editors, and publishers for such vaguely worded offenses as "insulting Islam" and "damaging the foundations of the Islamic Republic." Since 1997, more than 100 publications have been shut down by the judiciary and scores of journalists have been arrested—often held incommunicado for extended periods of time and convicted in closed-door trials. Circulation of pro-reform newspapers has fallen from a peak of more than three million to just over one million.

Scores of journalists were summoned for interrogation during the year, and dozens were detained, with the number of journalists behind bars reaching a high of 22 in July. The authorities greatly increased ad hoc press restrictions and gag orders banning media coverage of specific topics and events. When 135 members of parliament wrote an open letter in May calling on Ayatollah Ali Khamenei to apologize to the public for ignoring their wishes, not a single newspaper dared to publish it (though it circulated widely on the Web).

While journalists had been allowed in the past to report on demonstrations with few problems, on June 12 the Supreme National Security Council (SNSC) issued a decree prohibiting journalists from entering the university campus in Tehran to cover student demonstrations. Vigilantes beat several journalists who defied the order and confiscated their film and equipment. In the weeks after the June riots, eight journalists were arrested for allegedly inciting students to revolt. The SNSC also issued a decree prohibiting journalists from speaking with foreign Farsi-language news services, and a number of those alleged to have done so were prohibited from leaving the country during the year. A ban on publishing articles about Iranian-American relations has remained in effect since May 2002.

The rapid growth of Internet access in Iran—there are now an estimated three million users—and the tendency of newspapers closed by the judiciary to continue publishing online led the government to begin systematically censoring Internet content for the first time in 2003. In May, Internet service providers (ISPs) were instructed by the Ministry of Telecommunications to block access to a list of "immoral sites and political sites that insult the country's political and religious leaders." At least 12 ISPs were shut down during the year for failing to install filters against banned sites. At least three journalists were arrested in connection with material they published on the Internet.

Religious freedom is limited in Iran, which is 89 percent Shi'a Muslim and 10 percent Sunni Muslim. Sunnis enjoy equal rights under the law, but there are some indications of discrimination, such as the absence of a Sunni mosque in the Iranian capital and the paucity of Sunnis in senior government offices. The constitution recognizes Zoroastrians, Jews, and Christians as religious minorities and generally allows them to worship without interference, but they are barred from election to representative bodies (though a set number of parliamentary seats are reserved for them), cannot hold senior government or military positions, and face restrictions in employment, education, and property ownership. In February, Iran released the last 5 of 10 Jews convicted in a closed-door trial of spying for Israel in 2000. In December, the Expediency Council approved legislation equalizing the amount of "blood money" owed to families of Muslim and non-Muslim murder victims. Some 300,000 Baha'is, Iran's largest non-Muslim minority, enjoy virtually no rights under the law and are banned from practicing their faith. Hundreds of Baha'is have been executed since 1979.

Academic freedom in Iran is limited. Scholars are frequently detained for expressing political views and students involved in organizing protests often face suspension or expulsion by university disciplinary committees.

The constitution permits the establishment of political parties, professional syndicates, and other civic organizations, provided they do not violate the principles of "freedom, sovereignty and national unity" or question the Islamic basis of the republic. In 2002, the 44-year-old Iran Freedom Movement was banned on such grounds and 33 of its leading members imprisoned.

The 1979 constitution prohibits public demonstrations that "violate the principles of Islam," a vague provision used to justify the heavy-handed dispersal of assemblies and marches. According to Amnesty International, the authorities arrested up to 4,000 people during the June demonstrations, about half of whom were detained for more than a week, and charged at least 65 people with criminal offenses. Hundreds of students and political activists were arrested in July and August, including three leaders of the Office to Foster Unity (OFU) and four leaders of the Melli Mazhabi (National Religious Alliance).

In recent years, hardline vigilante organizations, most notably the Basij and Ansar-i Hezbollah, have played a major role in dispersing public demonstrations. Shortly after the outbreak of the June protests, Khamenei warned that "the Iranian nation" may "decide to take action against the rioters," a striking indication that such vigilante groups are sanctioned by the conservative establishment. During the year, at least seven reformist members of parliament were beaten or blocked from giving public speeches in cities outside of the capital.

Iranian law does not allow independent labor unions to exist, though workers' councils are represented in the government-sanctioned Workers' House, the country's only legal labor federation. While strikes and work stoppages are not uncommon, the authorities often ban or disperse demonstrations that criticize national economic policies. In 2003, the Ministry of the Interior prohibited the Worker's House from holding a demonstration on International Labor Day (May 1), citing regional tensions.

The judiciary is not independent. The Supreme Leader directly appoints the head of the judiciary, who in turn appoints senior judges. Civil courts provide some procedural safeguards, though judges often serve simultaneously as prosecutors during trials. Political and other sensitive cases are tried before Revolutionary Courts, where detainees are denied access to legal counsel and due process is ignored. The penal code is based on Sharia and provides for flogging, stoning, amputation, and death for a range of social and political offenses.

Iranian security forces subjected thousands of citizens to arbitrary arrest and incommunicado detention in 2003. Suspected dissidents are often held in unofficial, illegal detention centers, and allegations of torture are commonplace. Zahra Kazemi, a Canadian Iranian photo journalist, was arrested in June while taking photographs outside Tehran's high-security Evin prison and was beaten to death in custody.

There are few laws that discriminate against ethnic minorities, who are permitted to establish community centers and certain cultural, social, sports, and charitable associations. However, Kurdish demands for more autonomy and a greater voice in the appointment of a regional governor have not been met and some Kurdish opposition groups are brutally suppressed. At least two members of Komala, a Kurdish political organization affiliated with the Communist Party of Iran, were executed in 2003.

Although women enjoy the same political rights as men and currently hold several seats in parliament and even one of Iran's vice presidencies, they face discrimination in legal and social matters. A woman cannot obtain a passport without the permission of a male relative or her husband, and women do not enjoy equal rights under laws governing divorce, child custody disputes, or inheritance. A woman's testimony in court is given only half the weight of a man's. Women must conform to strict dress codes and are segregated from men in most public places. Several pieces of legislation intended to give women equal rights, such as a bill on divorce law that parliament approved in August 2002, have been rejected by the Council of Guardians. In November 2003, the Expediency Council approved a law giving divorced mothers the right to have custody of boys aged seven and under. The previous law automatically granted divorced fathers custody of male children over the age of two.

Iraq

Population: 24,200,000 **Political Rights:** 7
GNI/capita: $1,090 **Civil Liberties:** 5*
Life Expectancy: 58 **Status:** Not Free
Religious Groups: Muslim (97 percent), Christian or other (3 percent)
Ethnic Groups: Arab (75-80 percent), Kurd (15-20 percent). other [including Turkmen and Assyrian] (5 percent)
Capital: Baghdad
Ratings Change: Iraq's civil liberties rating improved from 7 to 5 due to the expansion of freedoms of expression and association.

Ten-Year Ratings Timeline (Political Rights, Civil Liberties, Status)

1994	1995	1996	1997	1998	1999	2000	2001	2002	2003
7,7NF	7,7NF	7,7NF	7,7NF	7,7NF	7,7NF	7,7NF	7,7NF	7,7NF	7,5NF

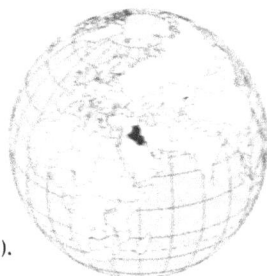

Overview: Following the April 2003 ouster of Saddam Hussein's tyrannical government by a U.S. and British military coalition, the Coalition Provisional Authority (CPA) presided over a sweeping expansion of civil liberties and began implementing an ambitious plan to establish a democratic government by the end of 2005. However, an escalating insurgency, supported by much of the country's once-dominant Sunni Arab minority, perpetuated a climate of instability and hampered reconstruction efforts.

The modern state of Iraq, consisting of three former Ottoman provinces, was established after World War I as a British-administered League of Nations mandate. In 1921, Britain installed a constitutional monarchy in which Sunni Arabs came to dominate most political and administrative posts at the expense of Kurds and Shiite Arabs. Sunni political dominance in Iraq, which formally gained independence in 1932, continued after the monarchy was overthrown in a 1958 military coup. Following a succession of weak leftist regimes, the pan-Arab Baath (Renaissance) party seized power in 1968. In 1979, the Baathist regime's de facto strongman, Saddam Hussein, formally assumed the presidency.

Hussein brutally suppressed all political opposition and sought to establish Iraq as a regional superpower by invading Iran in 1980. During the eight-year war, his regime used chemical weapons against both Iranian troops and rebellious Iraqi Kurds. Iraqi troops invaded Kuwait in 1990 and were ousted the following year by a U.S.-led coalition.

After the Gulf War, the UN Security Council imposed economic sanctions pending the destruction of Iraq's weapons of mass destruction (WMD). While it was originally anticipated that the sanctions would be lifted within a few years, Iraq refused to disclose its WMD capabilities for more than a decade and the sanctions remained in place. In the aftermath of the September 11, 2001 attacks on the United States, U.S. president George W. Bush designated Iraq's WMD a salient threat to American national security and committed his administration to engineering Hussein's ouster. In March 2003, U.S. and British forces invaded Iraq and captured Baghdad within three weeks.

The initial euphoria felt by many Iraqis in the immediate aftermath of the regime's collapse was soon tempered by the security vacuum, widespread looting, and acute electricity and water shortages that followed. Unemployment soared as a result of the CPA's early de-Baathification decrees, which left around 35,000 civil servants out of work, and the disbanding of Iraq's 400,000-man army. After extensive and often contentious negotiations with leading Iraqi political and religious leaders, the CPA appointed a 25-member Iraqi Governing Council (IGC) in July and granted it limited law-making authority. By year's end, however, decision making on major government policies remained in the hands of the CPA.

While care was taken to ensure that the composition of the IGC, as well as provisional local and regional government bodies, reflected Iraq's confessional and ethnic demography, Sunni Arabs viewed the diminution of their political supremacy with trepidation. Loose networks of Baath Party loyalists organized an insurgency in the "Sunni triangle" of central Iraq, which progressively gained strength during the year. Monthly combat fatalities suffered by coalition forces rose from 7 in May to a high of 94 in November, while terrorist attacks on government offices, humanitarian institutions, and civilian areas increased dramatically in the latter half of 2003. Several prominent Iraqis who supported the American occupation were assassinated during the year, including prominent Shiite clerics Abdel Majid Al-Khoei and Muhammad Baqir al-Hakim; IGC member Aquila Hashimi; the deputy mayor of Baghdad, Faris Abdul Razzaq al-Assam; and Mustafa Zaidan al-Khaleefa, a prominent member of a Baghdad neighborhood council. In response to the escalating violence, the CPA accelerated training of Iraqi security forces and relaxed its de-Baathification screening.

Although the CPA initially planned to restore Iraqi sovereignty only after a constitution was drafted and an elected Iraqi government was in place, the increased frequency and lethality of insurgent attacks led the United States to accelerate the transfer of power. Under a plan unveiled in November, the CPA and the IGC will be replaced in June 2004 by an unelected interim government, selected by provincial caucuses; an elected government will assume power by the end of 2005, after a constitution has been ratified. This new arrangement, which remains subject to change, was also intended to offer Sunni Arab leaders, who felt largely excluded from the IGC, a more substantial presence in the transitional assembly.

Several outbreaks of violence between Kurds and Turkmans in and around the northern city of Kirkuk occurred during the latter half of 2003, most notably a spate of clashes on August 24 that left 11 people dead.

Political Rights and Civil Liberties: Iraqis cannot yet change their government democratically, as the CPA wields virtually absolute authority, both directly and through its appointment of provisional government bodies. Nevertheless, the CPA consults regularly with political, religious, and tribal leaders in making decisions and has retracted some decrees that met with broad-based opposition.

Freedom of expression in Iraq is respected by the CPA, with some limits. Although domestic television broadcasting is dominated by the Iraqi Media Network (IMN), established in May 2003 by the CPA, independent print publications proliferated after the fall of Saddam Hussein's regime and are allowed to operate without significant interference. Satellite dishes, banned by the former regime, and unrestricted Internet access have become available to those who can afford them. Although critical of the CPA in many respects, a fact-finding mission sent to Iraq in June 2003 by the London-based Arab Press Freedom Watch (APFW) concluded that Iraqis are "free to think, write, print, publish, and distribute without fear and restrictions."

CPA Order 14 (June 2003) prohibits media organizations from publishing or broadcasting material that incites violence or civil disorder, advocates the return to power of the Baath Party, or contains statements that purport to be on behalf of the Baath Party. It also allows for the closure of media organizations that violate these regulations. At least three local media outlets—two newspapers and a radio station—were suspended during the year on such grounds. In November, the Dubai-based satellite TV news channel Al-Arabiya was banned from operating in Iraq after it broadcast an audiotape in which Saddam Hussein urged Iraqis to kill members of the provisional Iraqi government.

Twelve foreign journalists and other international media personnel were killed and two remained missing as a result of combat operations in Iraq in 2003. International human rights groups drew attention to the deaths of two journalists on April 8 by a U.S. tank returning hostile fire at a Baghdad hotel and the August 17 death of a reporter whose camera was mistaken for a rocket-propelled grenade launcher, claiming that internationally recognized rules of engagement were breached. Ahmed Shawkat, the editor of the liberal weekly *Bila Ittijah*, was gunned down by suspected Islamist militants in October. At least a dozen foreign journalists were detained, most of them briefly, by coalition forces and Iraqi police during the year, including several cameramen and photographers from Arab media outlets suspected of having advanced knowledge of insurgent attacks. In November, a Portuguese journalist was kidnapped in southern Iraq and held for ransom.

Islam is the state religion in Iraq and is likely to remain so under the new political system taking shape. Baathist-era restrictions on freedom of worship and controls over religious institutions have been lifted. Newly constructed Shiite mosques proliferated in the latter half of the year. Religious and ethnic groups in Iraq are represented in the IGC (which has 13 Shiites, 5 Sunni Arabs, 1 Christian and 1 Turkman) and civil service in proportion to their demographic strength. Most government restrictions on academic freedom have been abolished by the CPA, but some new limits have been imposed. De-Baathification of Iraq's universities led to the firing of more than sixteen hundred Baathist professors and other university employees in May, though some were later reinstated. While faculties were permitted to elect university administrators for the first time, nominees were vetted by the CPA.

Freedom of association and assembly are generally recognized by the CPA. Although the Baath Party has been banned, political organizations representing a wide range of viewpoints are allowed to organize freely. Public demonstrations, ranging from strikes by public sector workers to pro-Saddam rallies, occurred almost daily during the year without coalition interference. While coalition forces reportedly killed several unarmed demonstrators in 2003, most deaths appear to have resulted from soldiers returning fire at armed militants. Baathist-era laws banning worker strikes are no longer in effect.

The Iraqi judiciary is not independent. In June 2003, the CPA established the Judicial Review Committee to screen judges and prosecutors for past links to the Baath Party, involvement in human rights violations, and corruption, and to appoint replacements. Although Iraq's 1971 Criminal Procedure Code, which stipulates that suspects cannot be held more than 24 hours without an examining magistrate's ruling of sufficient evidence, remains in force and is generally observed in ordinary criminal cases, thousands of people suspected of security offenses were detained without charge by coalition troops and Iraqi police in 2003. At year's end, the CPA had roughly 12,800 such detainees in custody, including around 4,000 members of the Mujahedin-e Khalq Organization, an Iranian dissident group backed by the former Iraqi regime.

Relatives of detainees are rarely granted access to prisons, though most are eventually able to communicate with family members through handwritten messages exchanged through the International Committee of the Red Cross (ICRC). In November, coalition forces began detaining relatives of wanted men, including the wife and daughter of Izzat Ibrahim al-Douri, the former deputy head of the Baath party.

Public security for Iraqi women, who by some estimates constitute nearly 60 percent of the population, deteriorated significantly after the fall of the Baathist regime. In July 2003, Human Rights Watch reported that insecurity in major Iraqi cities and the "low priority" given to cases of sexual violence by police was preventing many female Iraqis from working and attending school. Islamist groups have used their newfound freedom to harassed unveiled women in many parts of the country. Although the CPA has pledged to protect and empower women, only three were appointed to the 25-member ICG and only one was given a ministerial position. In order to secure support from conservative and Islamist groups in Iraq, the CPA has declined to establish quotas for Iraqi women in the transitional assembly to be formed in 2004.

Israel

Population: 6,700,000 **Political Rights:** 1
[Note: includes about **Civil Liberties:** 3
220,000 Israeli settlers **Status:** Free
in the West Bank, about 20,000 in the Golan Heights.
and 7,500 in the Gaza Strip. Approximately 172,000 Jews
and 170,000 Arabs live in East Jerusalem.]
GNI/capita: $16,750
Life Expectancy: 79
Religious Groups: Jewish (80.1 percent), Muslim [mostly Sunni] (14.6 percent), Christian (2.1 percent), other (3.2 percent)
Ethnic Groups: Jewish (80 percent), non-Jewish [mostly Arab] (20 percent)
Capital: Jerusalem
Note: The numerical rating and status reflect the state of political rights and civil liberties within Israel itself. Separate reports examine political rights and civil liberties in the Israeli administered territories and in the Palestinian administered areas.

Ten-Year Ratings Timeline (Political Rights, Civil Liberties, Status)

1994	1995	1996	1997	1998	1999	2000	2001	2002	2003
1,3F	1,3F	1,3F	1,3F	1,3F	1,3F	1,3F	1,3F	1,3F	1,3F

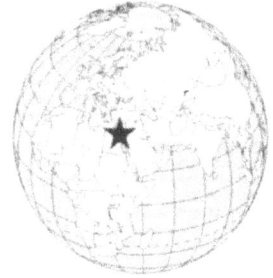

Overview: Israelis suffered greatly from Palestinian terrorism in 2003, even with a nearly two-month ceasefire. Several suicide bombings killed over 200 Israelis, eroding public security. The attacks elicited powerful Israeli reprisals against targets in the West Bank, Gaza Strip, and, for the first time in 30 years, Syria. Notwithstanding the crisis atmosphere, Israelis strived in 2003 to lead normal lives; they enjoyed and exercised substantial political freedom, and most Israelis—with the exception of the country's 20 percent Arab minority—enjoyed full civil rights. The government of Prime Minister Ariel Sharon of the Likud Party, after winning a landslide election early in the year, pushed ahead with construction of a controversial security barrier in the West Bank. The police launched investigations in response to an official inquiry into the shooting deaths of 13 Arab-Israeli citizens by Israeli police officers in 2000. Several Arab citizens and Arab residents of East Jerusalem were charged during the year with aiding and abetting radical Palestinian groups in suicide bomb attacks in Israel. Two joint Israeli-Palestinian nongovernmental peace initiatives garnered limited domestic support on both sides. In November, four former heads of Israel's internal security service warned that the government's strong-arm tactics against the Palestinians were endangering Israelis. Municipal elections in October were marred by hundreds of criminal investigations of local political activists. The government dismantled the Religious Affairs Ministry, further eroding the near-monopolistic control over religious life by the Orthodox establishment. The Israeli economy continued to suffer under the strain of combating terrorism; state subsidies for social programs were slashed, and workers staged several large-scale strikes.

Israel was formed in 1948 from less than one-fifth of the original British Palestine Mandate. Arab nations rejected a UN partition plan that would also have created a

Palestinian state. Immediately following Israel's declaration of independence, its neighbors attacked. While Israel maintained its sovereignty, Jordan seized East Jerusalem and the West Bank and Egypt took control of the Gaza Strip. In the 1967 Six-Day War, Israel came to occupy Sinai, the West Bank, Gaza, East Jerusalem, and the Golan Heights. Syria had previously used the Golan to shell towns in northern Israel. Israel annexed East Jerusalem in 1967 and the Golan Heights in 1981.

Prime Minister Yitzhak Rabin's Labor-led coalition government secured a breakthrough agreement with the Palestine Liberation Organization (PLO) in 1993. The Declaration of Principles, negotiated secretly between Israeli and Palestinian delegations in Oslo, Norway, provided for a phased Israeli withdrawal from the Israeli-occupied West Bank and Gaza Strip and for limited Palestinian autonomy in those areas, and for Palestinian recognition of Israel and a renunciation of terrorism. On November 4, 1995, a right-wing Jewish extremist, opposed to the peace process, assassinated Rabin in Tel Aviv.

At Camp David in July 2000 and at Taba, Egypt, in the fall and in early 2001, Prime Minister Ehud Barak and U.S. president Bill Clinton engaged the Palestinian leadership in the most far-reaching negotiations ever. For the first time, Israel discussed compromise solutions on Jerusalem, agreeing to some form of Palestinian sovereignty over East Jerusalem and Islamic holy sites in Jerusalem's Old City. Israel also offered all of the Gaza Strip and more than 95 percent of the West Bank to the Palestinians. However, the Palestinian leadership rejected the Israeli offers. Some analysts suggested that Yasser Arafat, chairman of the Palestinian Authority, was not satisfied that Palestinian territory in the West Bank would be contiguous and that Israel would recognize a "right of return," which would allow Palestinian refugees to live in Israel. Following a controversial visit by Likud Party leader Ariel Sharon to the Temple Mount in Jerusalem in September 2000, the Palestinians launched an armed uprising. Snap Israeli elections in February 2001 took place against the backdrop of continuing Palestinian violence. Sharon, promising Israelis both peace and security from terrorism, trounced Barak at the polls.

As Israelis prepared to go the polls for national elections in January 2003, two Arab members of the Knesset (parliament)—Ahmed Tibi and Azmi Bishara—were banned by Israel's Central Election Committee from running. Both were accused of opposing the existence of Israel as a Jewish state and encouraging Palestinian violence against Jews. The Israeli Supreme Court subsequently overturned the ban, allowing the two to run in the elections.

In late January, voters handed Sharon's Likud Party a landslide victory over the leading opposition Labor Party. Likud gained 37 seats, while Labor picked up only 19. Likud joined forces with the centrist Shinui Party, which gained 15 seats, and with two right-wing parties—the National Religious Party and the National Union Party—forming a comfortable coalition government with a total of 68 out of 120 Knesset seats. For the first time in Israel's history, an Arab citizen, Salah Tarif, was accorded a full cabinet portfolio.

Sharon's security platform helped divert voter attention from corruption scandals revealed on the eve of elections. Sharon was accused of conspiring with his sons to hide an illegal foreign loan to pay back an illegal foreign donation made to Sharon's campaign coffers. A vote-buying scandal implicating the Likud Party also failed to dissuade voters.

Palestinians carried out several devastating suicide bomb attacks inside Israel in 2003. The attacks, which took place inside buses, cafés, restaurants, bars, markets, shopping malls, and private homes, were random, occurring in large cities, smaller towns, and on kibbutzim. A suicide bombing by Hamas, a radical Palestinian group, aboard a Jerusalem bus in August killed 18 civilians, mostly Orthodox Jews returning from prayers at the Western Wall in Jerusalem's Old City. That attack violated a seven-week cease-fire arranged by radical Palestinian groups and the Palestinian Authority. After Israel retaliated by assassinating Hamas leaders, Hamas and Islamic Jihad called off the cease-fire, which had provided Israelis with an unusual stretch of relative calm and a return to some normalcy. Despite the attacks, Israelis carried on with their daily lives; citizens continued to ride public buses, eat in restaurants, and participate in public gatherings and events. Several suicide bombings were also prevented, including over 20 in November, according to Israeli security services.

In October, after an Islamic Jihad suicide bomber murdered 21 Israelis—including several Arabs—at a restaurant in Haifa, Israeli warplanes bombed a purported Islamic Jihad training camp in Syria. The attack marked the first time Israel had struck within Syria since the 1973 Yom Kippur War. The air strike increased tensions between the two countries; in late October, Syria's foreign minister threatened to attack Israeli civilian communities on the Golan Heights.

Palestinians in the Gaza Strip carried out several rocket and mortar attacks against Israeli town and cities to the north and east of the strip. The rockets were of a longer range than those fired in previous years, suggesting greater sophistication by the attackers and their acquisition of more advanced weaponry.

Israeli Defense Forces (IDF) retaliated for many terrorist attacks throughout the year. The IDF carried out targeted killings of terrorist suspects in the West Bank and Gaza, where it also staged air strikes, demolished private homes, and imposed curfews. The United States and other nations criticized Israel for the killings of innocent Palestinians, during Israeli antiterror operations.

Israeli reprisals for Palestinian attacks led to some divisions within the Israeli military. The air force grounded several active pilots who, concerned about harming innocent Palestinians, refused orders to attack suspects in the West Bank and Gaza.

In November, the IDF's chief of staff, Lieutenant General Moshe Ya'alon publicly criticized Sharon's policies, saying they were strengthening terrorist organizations and undermining moderate Palestinian politicians. General Ya'alon's remarks followed warnings by four former heads of the Shin Bet, Israel's domestic security service, that the government's policies were leading the country to "catastrophe." Tensions were high along Israel's northern border with Lebanon during the year. In August, Hezbollah, a radical Shiite Muslim group backed by Iran and Syria and based in southern Lebanon, shelled northern Israel, killing one person. After Israel's air strike against Syria in October, a Hezbollah sniper fired across the border into Israel, killing an IDF soldier. Hezbollah also shelled Israeli positions.

Hezbollah reportedly took delivery of rockets capable of striking Israeli population and industrial centers. The group has in the past attacked Israeli positions patrolling near the Shebba Farms area. Hezbollah considers the area occupied Lebanese territory, despite UN confirmation in June 2000 that Israel had withdrawn fully from the "security zone" in southern Lebanon it had occupied for 18 years. Israel had held the zone to protect its northern flank from attacks, including repeated Hezbollah rocketing of Israeli towns and farms.

Hezbollah continued to hold at least five Israeli hostages. Widely believed to be among them is Israeli airman Ron Arad, thought to be held in Lebanon or Iran since his plane was shot down over Lebanon in 1986. Hezbollah hinted during the year that it would negotiate for the hostages' release. Israel considered releasing hundreds of Arab prisoners in an exchange deal. There are more than 5,000 Palestinians in Israeli jails.

Peace talks with Syria did not take place during the year. Intensive negotiations broke down in January 2000 over disagreements on final borders around the Golan Heights.

The initiation of approximately 400 criminal investigations of local political activists on allegations of arson, vandalism, fraud, and other election-related malfeasance tainted municipal elections in October.

In the fall, a group of former Israeli and Palestinian politicians revealed a private peace initiative negotiated in secret in Geneva, Switzerland. Based largely on terms discussed by Israeli and Palestinian negotiators at Taba, Egypt, in December 2000-January 2001, the nongovernmental "Geneva accord" envisioned an independent Palestinian state in the West Bank and Gaza Strip, the dismantlement of Jewish settlements in those areas, the division of Jerusalem, and sole Palestinian control of the Temple Mount in Jerusalem's Old City with international monitoring. In return, Palestinians would pledge peace. There was also a vague reference to the Palestinians dropping their demand for a "right of return" of refugees to Israel. While the accord drew some limited support from the Israeli and Palestinian publics, their respective leaders largely ignored it. Another peace plan headed by former Shin Bet chief Ami Ayalon and Palestinian academic and peace activist Sari Nusseibeh also gathered limited support.

The Israeli economy suffered throughout the year from a drop in tourism and the strain of combating the Palestinian uprising. Finance Minister Benyamin Netanyahu instituted strict austerity measures, including budget reductions, layoffs, privatization schemes, and cuts in social security payments. A general strike called by Histadrut, the national labor union, paralyzed the country in April. Banks, school, and airports closed in response to the Treasury's plan to slash $2.3 billion from the state budget. In an effort to boost domestic employment, the government deported 30,000 foreign workers during the year.

A report released in October by the National Insurance Institute, a quasi-government agency, showed that 21 percent of Israelis live below the poverty line. Of 1.3 million said to be in poverty, more than 600,000 are children. Ultra-Orthodox Jews and non-Jews were the most vulnerable segments of the population.

Political Rights and Civil Liberties: Israeli citizens can change their government democratically. Although Israel has no formal constitution, a series of basic laws has the force of constitutional principles.

Arab residents of East Jerusalem, while not granted automatic citizenship, were issued Israeli identity cards after the 1967 Six-Day War. However, by law, Israel strips Arabs of their Jerusalem residency if they remain outside the city for more than three months. Arab residents have the same rights as Israeli citizens, except the right to vote in national elections. They do have the right to vote in municipal elections and are eligible to apply for citizenship. Many choose not to seek citizenship out of solidarity with Palestinians in the West Bank and Gaza Strip, and because they believe East Jerusalem should be the capital of an independent Palestinian state. East Jerusalem's Arab population does not receive a share of municipal services proportionate to its numbers. Arabs in East Jerusalem do have the right to vote in Palestinian Authority elections.

Press freedom is respected in Israel. Newspaper and magazine articles on security matters are subject to a military censor, though the scope of permissible reporting is wide. Editors may appeal a censorship decision to a three-member tribunal that includes two civilians. Arabic-language publications are censored more frequently than are Hebrew-language ones. Newspapers are privately owned and freely criticize government policy. In October, a pirate radio station, Arutz Sheva, was forced off the air by the government for operating without a license. The station, supportive of Jewish settlers in the West Bank and Gaza, broadcast from a boat in the Mediterranean Sea. In November, the Israeli Supreme Court upheld an appeal against a decision by the Israel Film Board to ban the screening of a documentary film critical of Israel's armed forces. Publishing the praise of violence is prohibited under the Counter-terrorism Ordinance. Israeli authorities prohibit expressions of support for groups that call for the destruction of Israel. Internet access is widespread.

Freedom of religion is respected. Each religious community has jurisdiction over its own members in matters of marriage, burial, and divorce. In the Jewish community, the Orthodox establishment generally handles these matters. As a result, the law does not allow civil marriages, which prevents a non-Jew from marrying a Jew. In February 2002, the Supreme Court for the first time formally recognized Jewish conversions performed by Reform and Conservative rabbis in Israel. While the ruling allows those converted by non-Orthodox rabbis to be listed as Jews in the official population registry, the Orthodox establishment can still refuse services to Reform and Conservative converts. In March 2003, the government ordered the indefinite suspension of the enforcement of the no-work law during the Jewish Sabbath. While the Orthodox community objected, Israel's large secular establishment celebrated the decision. Christians, Muslims, Bahais, and others enjoy freedom of religion.

In October, the Sharon cabinet disbanded the Religious Affairs Ministry, effectively putting rabbinic courts under control of the Justice Ministry. The decision cleared the way for increased allocations of state resources to non-Orthodox religious institutions, including those attached to the Reform and Conservative movements. The move was seen as a further erosion of the Orthodox monopoly on Israel's religious affairs.

There is widespread academic freedom in Israel, in the midst of which there are trends of growing polarization between right and left academics, including occasional reports of ad hominem attacks on both sides.

Freedom of assembly and association is respected. Demonstrations, including outside government buildings and official residences of the prime minister, are permitted. Israel features a vibrant civic society, which includes many nongovernmental organizations. Workers may join unions of their choice and enjoy the right to strike and to bargain collectively. Three-quarters of the workforce either belong to unions affiliated with Histadrut or are covered under its social programs and collective bargaining agreements. Foreign workers in the country legally enjoy wage protections, medical insurance, and guarantees against employer exploitation. Illegal workers are often at the mercy of employers, and many are exploited.

The judiciary is independent, and procedural safeguards are generally respected. Security trials, however, may be closed to the public on limited grounds. The Emergency Powers (Detention) Law of 1979 provides for indefinite administrative detention without trial. The policy stems from emergency laws in place since the creation of Israel. Most administrative detainees are Palestinian, but there are currently two Lebanese detainees being held on national security grounds. They are believed to have direct knowledge of missing Israeli airman Ron Arad.

In September, an independent commission issued its findings of a public inquiry into the shooting deaths of 13 Arab Israeli citizens by Israeli police in October 2000. The police opened fire on rioters demonstrating in support of the Palestinian uprising. The report focused carefully on discrimination against the Arab minority in Israel, calling it the primary cause of the riots in 2000. The report recommended censuring former Interior Minister Shlomo Ben-Ami and barring him from holding high office again. The report led to the initiation of criminal investigations of several of the police officers who had opened fire, labeling them "prejudiced." While the 800-plus-page report was criticized by some for not going far enough—and by others for excusing Arab violence—it was generally regarded as an important breakthrough in addressing the social and economic disparities between Jewish and Arab Israelis. Prime Minister Ariel Sharon announced that more Arab citizens would be integrated into Israel's business community; he appointed several Arab Israelis to the boards of state-owned companies.

Some Israeli analysts, including supporters of Arab minority rights, raised caution about radicalization of segments of Israel's Arab population and of Arab residents of East Jerusalem. Several Arab Israelis and East Jerusalem residents were arrested in 2003 for transporting Palestinian suicide bombers to their targets. Several other Arab Israelis, including the mayor of the Arab town of Uhm al-Fahm, were arrested in May on suspicion of channeling money to the radical Islamist group Hamas. Eight Jerusalem Arabs with suspected ties to Hamas were also arrested in May for planning a bus hijacking.

In July, the government passed a new law barring citizenship to Palestinians from the West Bank and Gaza who marry Arab Israelis. The law, which expires after one year, would ostensibly lead to the separation of families. The law is not retroactive; it would not affect Palestinians previously granted citizenship. Some human rights groups characterized the new law as racist. Israel said the law was necessary because some Palestinians have opportunistically married Arab citizens of Israel so they can move to the country and more easily carry out terrorist attacks.

Some one million Arab citizens (roughly 20 percent of the population) receive inferior education, housing, and social services relative to the Jewish population. Israeli Arabs are not subject to the military draft, though they may serve voluntarily. Those who do not join the army are not eligible for financial benefits—including scholarships and housing loans—available to Israelis who have served. Most Bedouin housing settlements are not recognized by the government and are not provided with basic infrastructure and essential services.

Freedom of movement is affected sometimes by security alerts and emergency measures that can subject Israelis to long waits at roadblocks and at public places. The Israeli government continued construction of a security barrier in the West Bank designed to prevent Palestinian suicide bombers from infiltrating Israel.

Women have achieved substantial parity at almost all levels of Israeli society. Women are somewhat under-represented in public affairs; 18 women sit in the 120-seat Knesset. In the May 1999 election, an Arab woman, Husaina Jabara, was elected to the Knesset for the first time. Arab women face some societal pressures and traditions that negatively affect their professional, political, and social lives. The trafficking of women has become a problem in recent years.

Jordan

Population: 5,500,000 **Political Rights:** 5*
GNI/capita: $1,750 **Civil Liberties:** 5
Life Expectancy: 69 **Status:** Partly Free
Religious Groups: Sunni Muslim (92 percent),
Christian (6 percent), other (2 percent)
Ethnic Groups: Arab (98 percent), other [including
Armenian] (2 percent)
Capital: Amman
Ratings Change: Jordan's political rights rating improved from 6 to 5 due to the restoration of an elected parliament.

Ten-Year Ratings Timeline (Political Rights, Civil Liberties, Status)

1994	1995	1996	1997	1998	1999	2000	2001	2002	2003
4,4PF	4,4PF	4,4PF	4,4PF	4,5PF	4,4PF	4,4PF	5,5PF	6,5PF	5,5PF

Overview:
Following King Abdullah's rule by decree for more than two years, reasonably free and transparent, though not fair, parliamentary and municipal elections were held in 2003. In addition, some restrictions on freedom of expression were lifted during the year, and women assumed a higher profile in the government. Nevertheless, it remains to be seen whether King Abdullah's promise of a "new era" of political and civil liberties will come to fruition. With substantial assistance from the United States and other outside donors, Jordan's economy remained strong in spite of the war in neighboring Iraq.

The Hashemite Kingdom of Jordan, known as Transjordan until 1950, was established as a League of Nations mandate under the control of Great Britain in 1921 and granted full independence in 1946. Following the assassination of King Abdullah in 1951, the crown passed briefly to his mentally unstable eldest son, Talal, and then to his grandson, Hussein. King Hussein's turbulent 46-year reign witnessed a massive influx of Palestinian refugees (who now comprise a majority of the population), the loss of all territory west of the Jordan River in 1967, and numerous assassination and coup attempts by Palestinian and Arab nationalists. Although the 1952 constitution provided for a directly elected parliament, political parties were banned in 1956, and parliament was either suspended entirely or emasculated by government intervention in the electoral process for over three decades. While political and civil liberties remained tightly restricted, Hussein proved adept at co-opting, rather than killing, jailing, or exiling, his political opponents. As a result, Jordan avoided the legacy of brutal repression characteristic of other authoritarian regimes in the Arab world.

As a result of the decline of oil revenues in 1980s, which translated into reduced aid and worker remittances from the Arab Gulf countries, Jordan borrowed heavily throughout the decade and was eventually forced to implement economic austerity measures in return for IMF assistance. In April 1989, price increases for fuel and other subsidized commodities provoked widespread rioting. In addition, internal pressure for greater freedom and representation mounted. In response, the government launched a rapid process of political liberalization. Free elections were held later that year, and restrictions on civil liberties were progressively eased. However, the reform process ground to a halt in the mid-1990s and suffered some reversals.

By the time of Hussein's death in February 1999 and the ascension of his son, Abdullah, the kingdom was again faced with severe economic problems. The "peace dividend" expected to follow from Jordan's 1994 peace treaty with Israel, in the form of improved trade with the West Bank and increased investment from Western Europe, had not filtered down to the population at large, which suffered from 27 percent unemployment. Faced with a crippling public debt, Abdullah launched economic reforms needed to attract international investment during the first two years of his rule.

The September 2000 outbreak of the al-Aqsa *intifada* (uprising) in the West Bank and Gaza had an enormous impact on the country, inflaming anti-Israeli sentiments among Jordanians of Palestinian descent, leftists, and Islamists, who dominate much of civil society. As the violence next door continued unabated, the Professional Associations Council (PAC) formed an anti-normalization committee to spearhead mass demonstrations demanding the annulment of Jordan's peace treaty with Israel.

The government reacted by suppressing criticism of Jordanian relations with Israel and banning all demonstrations. In 2001, Abdullah dissolved parliament, postponed general elections scheduled for November, and replaced elected municipal councils with state-appointed local committees. For more than two years, King Abdullah ruled by decree, and issued over 200 "temporary laws," exempt from legislative approval until parliament is reconvened, imposing new restrictions on freedom of expression and assembly, weakening due process protections, and promulgating economic policies that would have almost certainly have been rejected by the outgoing parliament.

As the United States readied for an invasion of Iraq in early 2003, many domestic and foreign observers questioned whether Jordan could cope with the war's fallout. The population's pro-Saddam sympathies, already pronounced during the 1991 Gulf War, had been reinforced in the 1990s by Iraq's shipments of discounted petroleum and preferential access given to Jordanian exports under the UN oil-for-food program. With anti-American sentiment at a peak and more than 400,000 Iraqis living and working in Jordan, the kingdom's decision to allow U.S. troops to operate on Jordanian soil appeared to carry enormous political and security risks. However, an infusion of "oil grants" from the Arab Gulf states and an additional $700 million in economic assistance from the United States (above and beyond its annual $250 million aid package) helped the kingdom avoid an economic crisis, while royal promises to undertake postwar political liberalization persuaded mainstream opposition groups to refrain from mobilizing the public against the government's pro-American alignment. As a result, while the government forcibly dispersed unlicensed demonstrations and detained several antiwar activists for much of the conflict, its suppression of antiwar dissent was far less heavy-handed than that of other pro-U.S. regimes in the Arab world. Within two weeks of the fall of Baghdad in April 2003, Abdullah scrapped a 2001 decree restricting freedom of the press and pledged to hold "free and impartial" parliamentary elections in June.

Although gerrymandering favored representatives of tribes and families traditionally loyal to the Hashemite monarchy, the June parliamentary elections were largely free of fraud. Supervision of elections was transferred from the Interior Ministry to the judiciary, ballots were counted directly at polling stations rather than at a center run by the Interior Ministry, and registered voters were required to produce new identity cards with magnetic strips in order to receive ballots. However, some women may have been deterred from voting by the government's refusal to station female election monitors at polling centers, making it necessary for veiled women to reveal their faces to male monitors before entering polling booths. The Central Elections Committee rejected the applications of two opposition candidates on weak grounds. All major political groups participated in the poll, including the Islamic Action Front (IAF), which captured 16 seats. However, the newly elected parliament has yet to overturn most temporary laws restricting political and civil liberties. In October, King Abdullah unexpectedly replaced Prime Minister Ali Abul Ragheb with Faisal al-Fayez, the minister for the royal court, and unveiled a new cabinet of mostly American- and British-educated technocrats, including three women.

Although municipal elections were held in July, a new law empowering the government to appoint mayors and half of all municipal council seats—a restriction previously imposed only on municipal government in the capital—led the IAF and other opposition groups to boycott the polls in most districts.

Political Rights and Civil Liberties: Jordanians cannot change their government democratically. The king holds broad executive powers and may dissolve parliament and dismiss the prime minister or cabinet at his discretion. The 110-seat lower house of parliament, elected through universal adult suffrage, may approve, reject, or amend legislation proposed by the cabinet, but is restricted in its ability to initiate legislation and cannot enact laws without the assent of the 55-seat upper house of parliament, which is appointed by the king. Regional governors are appointed by the central government, as are half of all municipal council seats.

The electoral system in Jordan is heavily skewed toward the monarchy's traditional support base. The single-member-district system, introduced in 1993, favors tribal and family ties over political and ideological affiliations, while rural districts with populations of Transjordanian origin are over-represented relative to urban districts, where most Jordanians of Palestinian descent reside (according to the *Financial Times*, Amman has a member of parliament for every 52,255 voters, while the small town of Karak has an MP for every 6,000 voters). In 2003, only 27 percent of registered voters went to the polls in Amman, a possible indication that many Palestinian Jordanians still feel excluded from the political system.

Freedom of expression is restricted. The state owns all broadcast media and has wide discretionary powers to close print publications. In April, the government repealed Article 150 of the Penal Code, an amendment promulgated by royal decree in 2001 that empowered the State Security Court (SSC) to close publications and imprison individuals for up to three years for publishing information deemed harmful to national unity or the reputation of the state. In January, prior to the repeal of Article 150, the editor in chief, managing editor, and a writer for the weekly *Al-Hilal* were arrested for publishing an article "lacking respect for the family of the Prophet Muhammad" and sentenced by the SSC the following month to prison sentences of two to six months; two of the sentences were commuted to fines, but the author of the article went to jail. The Information Ministry was scrapped in October, and regulation of the media is now the responsibility of an appointed Higher Media Council. Although the law still allows journalists to be jailed by the civilian judiciary, government officials have pledged that journalists will no longer be sent to prison for their writings.

There is no official advance censorship in Jordan, but the authorities are usually tipped off about the contents of potentially offensive articles by informers at printing presses, and editors are then forced to remove the articles. In 2003, the authorities ordered the independent weekly *Al-Wehda* to remove an article about torture in Jordanian prisons from its September 24 issue; when the paper refused, the entire issue was banned. In November, *Al-Wehda* complied with an order to remove a caricature of Fayez and his newly appointed cabinet before its issue hit newsstands. The government has not attempted to censor Internet content. However, government monitoring of telephone conversations and Internet communication is reportedly common.

Islam is the state religion. The government appoints all Islamic clergy, pays their salaries, and monitors sermons at mosques, where political activity is banned under Jordanian law. Sunni Muslims constitute 92 percent of the population, but Christians and Jews are officially recognized as religious minorities and allowed to worship freely. Baha'is and Druze are allowed to practice their faiths, but are not officially recognized. Academic freedom is generally respected in Jordan.

Freedom of assembly is heavily restricted. A temporary law on public gatherings, introduced in August 2001, bans demonstrations lacking written consent from the government. Although the government allowed a number of licensed antiwar demonstrations to take place before and during the U.S.-led invasion of Iraq in March 2003, at least 16 antiwar campaigners were arrested in the weeks leading up to the war, and security forces forcibly dispersed unlicensed demonstrations that erupted after the war began, detaining dozens of protestors. By the end of the war, all had been released and none were charged with criminal offenses. Nongovernmental organizations (NGOs) are routinely licensed in Jordan, and dozens of NGOs address numerous political and social issues. However, professional associations have come under pressure to abstain from political activities. Workers have the right to bargain collectively, but must receive government permission to strike. More than 30 percent of the workforce is organized into 17 unions.

The judiciary is subject to executive influence through the Justice Ministry and the Higher Judiciary Council, whose members are appointed by the king. While most trials in civilian courts are open and procedurally sound, proceedings of the SSC are closed to the public. A temporary law promulgated in 2001 allows the prime minister to refer any case to the SSC and denies the right of appeal to people convicted of misdemeanors, which can carry short prison sentences.

Jordanian citizens enjoy little protection from arbitrary arrest and detention. Under the constitution, suspects may be detained for up to 48 hours without a warrant and up to 10 days without formal charges being filed, but courts routinely grant prosecutors 15-day extensions of this deadline. Even these minimal protections are denied to suspects referred to the SSC, who are often held in lengthy pretrial detention and refused access to legal council until just before trial. Defendants charged with security-related offenses frequently allege that torture is used to extract confessions.

Jordanians of Palestinian descent face discrimination in employment by the government and the military and in admission to universities. Labor laws do not protect foreign workers. Abuse of mostly South Asian domestic servants is widespread.

Women enjoy equal political rights, but face legal discrimination in matters of inheritance and divorce, which fall under the jurisdiction of Sharia (Islamic law) courts, and in the provision of government pensions and social security benefits. Although women constitute only 14 percent of the workforce, the government has made efforts to increase the number of women in the civil service. Women are guaranteed a quota of six seats in parliament. Although the government repealed a law providing for lenient treatment of those convicted of "honor crimes" (the murder or attempted murder of women by relatives for alleged sexual misconduct), the newly elected lower house of parliament rejected the decree in August and rejected an amended version the following month. A royal decree granting women the right to initiate divorce proceedings was also rejected by parliament. In November, King Abdullah appointed seven women to the 55-seat upper house of parliament.

Kuwait

Population: 2,400,000   **Political Rights:** 4
GNI/capita: $18,270   **Civil Liberties:** 5
Life Expectancy: 78   **Status:** Partly Free
Religious Groups: Muslim (85 percent) [Sunni
70 percent, Shi'a 30 percent], other (15 percent)
Ethnic Groups: Kuwaiti (45 percent), other Arab (35 percent),
South Asian (9 percent), Iranian (4 percent), other (7 percent)
Capital: Kuwait City

Ten-Year Ratings Timeline (Political Rights, Civil Liberties, Status)

1994	1995	1996	1997	1998	1999	2000	2001	2002	2003
5,5PF	5,5PF	5,5PF	5,5PF	5,5PF	4,5PF	4,5PF	4,5PF	4,5PF	4,5PF

Overview: The war in Iraq dominated headlines in Kuwait during the first four months of 2003, as the U.S. military used Kuwaiti territory as the main staging area for its ground war against

Iraq in March and April. Despite tensions created by the American military presence, terrorist threats, a handful of missile attacks from Iraqi forces, and a spate of attacks against the American presence, Kuwait was able to maintain law and order during a tense period. On July 5, Kuwait held the tenth elections since independence for its 50-member National Assembly.

The al-Sabah family has played a role in ruling Kuwait for more than 200 years. A year after Kuwait gained its independence in 1961 from Britain, a new constitution gave broad powers to the emir and created the National Assembly. The emir has suspended the National Assembly two times in the last 40 years, from 1976 to 1981 and from 1986 to 1992.

After its restoration in 1992, parliament played an active role in monitoring the emir and the government, forcing government ministers out of office and blocking legislation proposed by the royal family. Parliament, however, has also served as an impediment to progressive political change, rejecting measures that would have granted women the right to vote and accelerated economic reforms.

The 2003 legislative elections did not meet minimal international standards, tainted by the exclusion of women from voting and allegations of widespread government-subsidized vote buying. Pro-government candidates with strong tribal backing did well in the elections, and candidates aligned with Islamists realized some slight gains. Out of 16 liberal candidates, only 3 managed to win seats, a decline of 4 seats from the previous National Assembly. Several analysts contend that the coalition of Islamists and pro-government members with conservative tribal ties may oppose measures to promote women's rights and full political participation, privatize the economy, and update investment laws.

Following the elections, Sabah al-Ahmad al-Sabah, half-brother of Emir Jaber al-Ahmad al-Sabah, became prime minister, taking over for ailing Saad al-Abdallah al-Sabah, who remains the crown prince. Sabah al-Ahmad al-Sabah's appointment as prime minister marks the first time since Kuwait's independence that the prime minister has not been the crown prince. The al-Sabah ruling dynasty is currently led by aging family members; the emir and crown prince are all in their seventies, and unanswered succession questions linger.

The 2002-2003 buildup of American military forces in Kuwait, which served as a staging ground for the land war against Iraq, led to internal tensions and a spate of attacks against American forces. Kuwait designated over half of its territory to serve as staging territory for U.S. forces, and it also donated in-kind assistance such as fuel to the war effort.

In October, the cabinet approved a measure that would allow women to stand for office and vote in municipal council elections. The measure still needs approval from the all-male National Assembly, which has in the past blocked government proposals to open the door to women's full participation in political life.

Political Rights and Civil Liberties: Freely elected representatives do not determine the policies of Kuwait's government. The royal family of Kuwait, which is a hereditary emirate, largely sets the government's policy agenda. The country's emir has overriding power in the political system, appointing the prime minister and cabinet. Under the constitution, the emir holds executive power and shares legislative power with the 50-member National Assembly, which is elected by a limited popular vote involving only about 15 percent of the country's 860,000 citizens. The emir has the power to dissolve the National Assembly at will but must call elections within 60 days. The National Assembly is granted powers to overturn decrees from the emir issued during a period when the assembly is not in session, and the assembly has exercised this power in a number of cases. The National Assembly can veto the appointment of the country's prime minister, but then it must choose from three alternates put forward by the emir. Kuwaiti male citizens have only a limited ability to change their government. Women are completely excluded from the political process.

The government bans formal political parties, but it has allowed political groupings such as parliamentary blocs to emerge. The al-Sabah family dominates political life and controls meaningful power. Although the 1962 constitution provides men and women with equal rights, only men aged 21 or over can vote and run for office, according to the current election law.

The government, which owns all broadcast media, places restrictions on freedom of expression. However, it sometimes allows open criticism and debate on politics in the press. Overall, journalists in Kuwait enjoy greater freedom than do some of their regional counterparts, but the government continues to enforce laws that prohibit direct criticism of the emir and senior members of the royal family. In June, the government charged Mohammed Jassem, the editor of *Al-Watan* newspaper and an advocate for political reform, with challenging the authority of and "uttering abusive statements" about the emir. Irritated by satellite television station Al-Jazeera, the government closed the station's offices in Kuwait City.

Kuwaitis have access to the Internet, though Internet service providers have blocked access to certain sites. In May, the Ministry of Communications conducted raids on numerous Internet cafes on the basis that they were not blocking sites deemed immoral by Islamic members of the National Assembly. The Ministry of Communication issued new regulations that require Internet cafe owners to collect the names and civil identification numbers of customers.

Islam is the state religion, and religious minorities are generally permitted to practice their religion freely in private. Academic freedom is generally respected, though some exercise self-censorship. Kuwait has a tradition of allowing relatively open and free private discussions, often conducted in traditional gatherings called *diwayniyas,* and usually only including men.

The government restricts freedom of assembly and protest, and public gatherings require government approval. Kuwait does not have a single legally recognized independent human rights organization, and the civil society sector is small. Workers have the right to join labor unions, but the government restricts freedom of association by mandating that there only be one union per occupational trade.

Kuwait lacks a truly independent judiciary. The emir appoints all judges, and the executive branch of government approves judicial promotions and renewals of judicial appointments. According to Kuwaiti law, authorities may detain suspects for four days without charge. The Ministry of the Interior supervises the main internal security forces, including the national police, the Criminal Investigation Division, and the Kuwait State Security.

An estimated 80,000 stateless residents, known as *bidoon*, are considered illegal residents and do not have full citizenship rights.

Citizens have the right to own property and establish businesses. Oil dominates the economy, accounting for at least 85 percent of public revenues. In the coming year, one thorny issue of contention between the National Assembly and the government is Project Kuwait, a proposal to invite foreign oil majors to develop the emirate's northern oilfields. Lawmakers are seeking provisions that would prevent foreigners from gaining any substantial control over Kuwait's main national resource.

Women face discrimination in several areas of society and remain under-represented in the workforce, although they have made recent gains. According to recent statistics, women account for 34 percent of the workforce and receive two-thirds of the bachelor's degrees in Kuwait. Women have been fighting for full political participation for decades, but have been blocked by conservative male political leaders and Islamist groups.

Lebanon

Population: 4,200,000 **Political Rights:** 6
GNI/capita: $4,010 **Civil Liberties:** 5
Life Expectancy: 73 **Status:** Not Free
Religious Groups: Muslim [Mostly Shi'a] (70 percent),
Christian (30 percent)
Ethnic Groups: Arab (95 percent), Armenian (4 percent),
other (1 percent)
Capital: Beirut

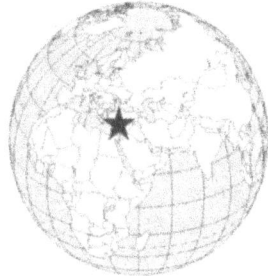

Ten-Year Ratings Timeline (Political Rights, Civil Liberties, Status)

1994	1995	1996	1997	1998	1999	2000	2001	2002	2003
6,5NF	6,5NF	6,5NF	6,5NF	6,5NF	6,5NF	6,5NF	6,5NF	6,5NF	6,5NF

Overview:
During 2003, Syria carried out two major troop redeployments, reducing its occupation force in Lebanon to fewer than 20,000 soldiers. However, its firm control of Lebanon's government continued to be the greatest impediment to freedom in Lebanon. The state's reaction to several major corruption scandals and security incidents during the year highlighted its continuing inability to investigate alleged wrongdoing by allies of Syria.

For more than a thousand years, the rough terrain of Mount Lebanon attracted Christian and heterodox-Muslim minorities fleeing persecution in the predominantly Sunni Muslim Arab world. After centuries of European protection and relative autonomy under Turkish rule, Mount Lebanon and its surrounding areas were established as a French mandate in 1920. After winning its independence in 1943, the new state of Lebanon maintained a precarious democratic system based on the division of parliamentary seats, high political offices, and senior administrative positions among the country's 17 officially recognized sectarian communities. As emigration transformed Lebanon's slight Christian majority into a minority, Muslim leaders demanded amendments to the fixed 6-to-5 ratio of Christian-to-Muslim parliamentary seats and to exclusive Maronite Christian control of the presidency. In 1975, war erupted between a coalition of Lebanese Muslim and leftist militias aligned with Palestinian guerrilla groups on one side and an array of Christian militias bent on preserving Christian political privileges on the other.

After the first few years of fighting, a loose consensus emerged among Lebanese politicians regarding a new power-sharing arrangement. However, following the entry of Syrian and Israeli troops into Lebanon in 1976 and 1978, the various militias and their foreign backers had little interest in disarming. The civil war lost much of its sectarian character over the next decade, with the bloodiest outbreaks of fighting taking place mainly within the Shiite, Christian, and Palestinian communities. Outside forces played a more direct role in the fighting. The Syrians battled Israeli forces in 1982, attacked a Palestinian-Islamist coalition in the mid-1980s, and fought the Lebanese army in 1989 and 1990, while the Israelis combated Palestinian and Shiite groups.

In 1989, the surviving members of Lebanon's 1972 parliament convened in Taif, Saudi Arabia, and agreed to a plan put forward by the Arab League that weakened the presidency, established equality in Christian and Muslim parliamentary representation, and mandated close security cooperation with occupying Syrian troops. After the ouster of General Michel Aoun from east Beirut by Syrian forces in October 1990, a new Syrian-backed government extended its writ throughout most of the country.

Over the next 12 years, Syria consolidated its control over Lebanese state institutions, particularly the presidency, the judiciary, and the security forces. However, in return for tacit Western acceptance of its control of Lebanon, Damascus permitted a degree of political and civil liberties in Lebanon that exceeded those in most other Arab countries. While those who directly criticized the occupation risked arbitrary arrest and imprisonment, criticism of the government was largely tolerated. The motley assortment of militia chiefs, traditional elites, and nouveaux riches who held civilian political positions in postwar Lebanon were persuaded to accept continued Syrian hegemony, primarily through a system of institutionalized corruption fueled by massive deficit spending on reconstruction during the 1990s. By the end of that decade, Lebanon's government debt exceeded its own gross national product and the economy was in deep recession.

As a result of this dismal economic downturn, vocal opposition to the Syrian presence began spreading across the political and sectarian spectrum. Mass demonstrations against the occupation grew in size and frequency throughout 2000 and 2001, while traditional Christian political and religious leaders, who had previously been silent about the issue, began denouncing it openly. Syria downsized its military presence in 2001, but demands for a complete pullout persisted.

After the September 11, 2001, attacks on the United States, Western pressure to preserve civil liberties subsided, in exchange for Syrian and Lebanese cooperation in the war against al-Qaeda. A number of unprecedented measures were taken to stifle freedom in 2002. Security forces closed an independent television station that had given voice to political dissidents, the government invalidated an opposition victory in a parliamentary by-election, and several opposition figures were placed under investigation for alleged ties to Israel and other foreign powers.

In April 2003, Damascus appointed a new cabinet widely seen as more solidly pro-Syrian. A deadlock between allies of Prime Minister Rafiq Hariri and President

Emile Lahoud paralyzed government decision making on important economic matters. The year witnessed a number of unresolved corruption scandals, most notably in connection with a debt crisis at Electricite du Liban, a state-owned company that provides power to most of the country, and the collapse in July of Bank al-Madina.

Numerous politically related security incidents occurred during the year, all of which remained conspicuously unsolved. In June, Prime Minister Hariri's television station was damaged by rockets. In July, political opposition figures traveling to a luncheon in the hometown of Interior Minister Elias Murr came under machine-gun fire and were forced to turn back. Later that month, the wife of Johnny Abdo, a former intelligence chief and presidential aspirant, was assaulted.

Political Rights and Civil Liberties: The Lebanese people have only a limited capacity to choose their own government. The Lebanese president is formally selected every six years by the 128-member parliament. In practice, however, this choice is made after Syrian authorization, known as "the password" in the Lebanese media. Syria and its allies also influence parliamentary and municipal elections more indirectly. The distribution of parliamentary seats is skewed in favor of regions where Syrian forces have been stationed the longest, such as the Beqaa Valley, and electoral districts are blatantly gerrymandered to ensure the election of pro-Syrian politicians. There has also been widespread interference during the elections themselves, with Lebanese security forces often present inside the polls. Prior to the June 2002 by-election in Metn, Interior Minister Elias Murr declared that using voting booth curtains to ensure secrecy was "optional," a remarkably blatant move to facilitate vote buying. A September 2003 by-election in the Baabda-Aley district was relatively free and fair, but local monitors reported some irregularities.

Political corruption in Lebanon is widely considered to be the most egregious in the Arab world. Transparency International listed Lebanon as the most corrupt of 11 Middle Eastern and North African countries surveyed in its 2003 Corruption Perceptions Index.

Lebanon has a long tradition of press freedom. Five independent television stations and more than 30 independent radio stations operate in Lebanon, though they are owned by prominent political and commercial elites. Dozens of independent print publications reflect a diverse range of views. Internet access is not restricted. However, in September 1991, the government signed a treaty with its larger neighbor explicitly pledging to "ban all political and media activity that might harm" Syria. This treaty, and a variety of subsequent laws drafted to comply with it, allows judges to censor foreign publications and to indict journalists for critical reporting on Syria, the Lebanese military, the security forces, the judiciary, and the presidency. In practice, such laws are mainly used to pressure the media into exercising self-censorship and rarely result in the imprisonment of journalists or the closure of media outlets. However, journalists who persistently violate taboos can be indicted and imprisoned on more serious charges. Permanent closure of licensed media outlets was rare until the closure of Murr Televisions (MTV) in 2002, which generated palpable anxiety among media owners of all political persuasions. MTV's appeal of the decision was rejected in April 2003.

Lebanese University professor Adonis Akra, the author of a newly published book about his experience in detention during an August 2001 crackdown against anti-Syrian activists, was indicted in February 2003 on charges of tarnishing the reputation of the judiciary and harming relations with Syria, and Dar al-Talia, the publishing house that printed the book, was shut down. On July 17, Amer Mashmoushi, the managing editor of the daily *Al-Liwa*, was indicted on charges of defaming the president after criticizing his handling of the Bank al-Madina scandal.

Freedom of religion is guaranteed in the Lebanese constitution and protected in practice, though sectarianism is formally enshrined in the political system. Nearly 350,000 Palestinian refugees living in Lebanon are denied citizenship rights and face restrictions on working, building homes, and purchasing property. Academic freedom is long-standing and firmly entrenched. The country's universities are the region's most open and vibrant.

Freedom of association and assembly is restricted. Although political parties are legal, a 1994 ban on the Christian Lebanese Forces (LF) party remains in place. Nongovernmental organizations, including human rights groups, are permitted to operate freely. Public demonstrations are not permitted without prior approval from the Interior Ministry, which does not rule according to uniform standards, and security forces routinely beat and arrest those who demonstrate against the Syrian occupation. Clashes between police and student activists occurred periodically throughout the year. Police forcibly dispersed a May 3 demonstration against the occupation using water cannons and batons, injuring 7 protestors and detaining 15 people.

All workers except those in government may establish unions, and all have the right to strike and to bargain collectively. Several major strikes occurred in 2003.

The judiciary is strongly influenced by Syrian political pressure, which affects the appointments of key prosecutors and investigating magistrates. The judicial system consists of civilian courts, a military court, and a judicial council. International standards of criminal procedure are not observed in the military court, which consists largely of military officers with no legal training, and cases are often tried in a matter of minutes. In recent years, the nominally independent Beirut Bar Association (BBA) has become less willing to confront the judiciary, allegedly because of widespread corruption. Muhamad Mugraby, a prominent human rights attorney who launched a campaign for "judicial integrity," was disbarred by the BBA in January 2003. After continuing to practice law, he was arrested in August on charges of "impersonating a lawyer" and detained for three weeks.

Arbitrary arrests and detentions by Lebanese (and, occasionally, Syrian) security forces are commonplace, and both have used torture in the past to extract confessions. It is widely known that the Syrian-controlled security agencies monitor the telephones of both cabinet ministers and political dissidents. Dozens of Islamist militants were arrested in 2003 on national security grounds. In May 2003, Hanna Chalita, a Christian political activist, was arrested by Syrian forces at the Lebanese-Syrian border and detained for more than a week. In July, one of the scores of Lebanese political prisoners still held by Syria, Joseph Huways, died in custody after reportedly being denied medical treatment.

Foreign domestic workers are exploited routinely and physically abused by employers. Women enjoy most of the same rights as men, but suffer social and some legal discrimination. Since family and personal status matters are adjudicated by the religious authorities of each sectarian community, Muslim women are subject to discriminatory laws governing marriage, divorce, inheritance, and child custody. Women are underrepresented in politics, holding only three parliamentary seats and no cabinet positions, and do not receive equal social security provisions and other benefits. Men convicted of so-called honor crimes against women usually receive lenient sentences.

Libya

Population: 5,500,000
GNI/capita: $5,944
Life Expectancy: 76
Religious Groups: Sunni Muslim (97 percent),
other (3 percent)
Ethnic Groups: Arab-Berber (97 percent), other [including
Greek, Italian, Egyptian, Pakistani, Turkish, Indian] (3 percent)
Capital: Tripoli

Political Rights: 7
Civil Liberties: 7
Status: Not Free

Ten-Year Ratings Timeline (Political Rights, Civil Liberties, Status)

1994	1995	1996	1997	1998	1999	2000	2001	2002	2003
7,7NF	7,7NF	7,7NF	7,7NF	7,7NF	7,7NF	7,7NF	7,7NF	7,7NF	7,7NF

Overview:
Libya made significant progress in its bid to break out from international isolation with the lifting of UN sanctions in September 2003. Despite limited cooperation from Libya on the war against terrorism, the U.S. government opted to maintain its unilateral sanctions against Libya, citing concerns with Libya's possible development of weapons of mass destruction, its lingering ties to terrorism, and its abysmal human rights record. In June, Libyan leader Mu'ammar al-Qadhafi appointed a new prime minister and announced broad economic reforms.

Libyan independence dates to 1951, when King Idris assumed power following a UN resolution establishing Libya as an independent and sovereign state. French and British forces had occupied Libya during World War II. Prior to the Allied occupation, Libya had been an Italian colony since an invasion in 1912. In the previous centuries, Libya was under Ottoman rule.

In 1969, Colonel Qadhafi seized power at the age of 25 in a military coup that deposed the staunchly pro-West King Idris. Qadhafi railed against Western control of Libya's oil fields and the presence of foreign military bases in Libya. He ushered in a highly personalized style of rule that combines elements of pan-Arabism with Islamic ideals. Qadhafi purported to find a "third way" that rejects both Western-style democracy and communism.

In the years following Qadhafi's rise to power, Libya gained international pariah status with its sponsorship of various acts of terrorism, as well as its support of insurgencies throughout sub-Saharan Africa. During the 1980s, Libyan meddling in the war in neighboring Chad proved to be a costly military failure. Libyan involvement in the 1988 bombing of Pan Am flight 103 over Lockerbie, Scotland, led the United Nations to impose sanctions on Libya in 1992. The sanctions included embargoes on air traffic and the import of arms and oil production equipment. The United States has maintained its own sanctions against Libya since 1981, citing Libyan sponsorship of terrorism.

Beginning in 1999, Qadhafi embarked on a strategy aimed at ending Libya's international isolation. He surrendered two Libyan nationals suspected in the Pan Am 103 bombing and agreed to compensate families of victims of the 1989 bombing of a French airliner over Niger. The Libyan government also accepted responsibility for the 1984 death of British police officer Yvonne Fletcher, killed by shots fired from the Libyan embassy in London. Qadhafi also expelled members of the Palestinian terrorist organization headed by Abu Nidal.

In response to Libya's surrendering of two terrorism suspects, the United Nations opted to suspend sanctions against Libya in 1999, although the permanent lifting of sanctions was withheld pending Libya's unequivocal renunciation of terrorism. The United States eased some of its restrictions by allowing for the limited sale of food and medicines to Libya, but maintained its travel ban as well as other restrictions. Britain opted to resume diplomatic ties with Libya, reopening its embassy in Tripoli in March 2001. The European Union followed suit by lifting sanctions, but maintains an arms embargo.

The two terrorism suspects went on trial in March 2000 at the International Court of Justice in the Netherlands, but under Scottish law. One of the suspects was found guilty of murder in January 2001 and sentenced to life imprisonment, while the other suspect was acquitted of all charges and freed. Following the trial, the United States and Britain repeated demands that Libya formally accept responsibility for the bombing, compensate the victims' families, and renounce terrorism.

In August 2003, the Libyan government struck a deal with the families of the Pan Am 103 bombing victims, offering to pay $2.7 billion in compensation. The victims' families will be awarded roughly $10 million each. In response, the United Nations voted to lift sanctions on Libya in September, removing a significant hurdle to Libya's reintegration into the global community. The Libyan government remains deadlocked with the French families of the victims of the 1989 UTA airliner bombing over Niger. Libya has already paid a total of $33 million to the victims' families and proposed to pay an additional $1 million per family, but the UTA families have said the compensation package is still too low.

The U.S. government continues to maintain unilateral sanctions against Libya. Washington remains concerned about Libya's potential links to terrorism as well as its long-range missiles and chemical weapons programs. These sanctions include a prohibition of U.S. investment in Libya, a ban on U.S. oil companies doing business in Libya, and a travel ban that forbids the use of American passports for travel to Libya. Libya has also remained on the U.S. government's list of state sponsors of terrorism. In addition, the United States maintains a freeze on Libyan assets. U.S. officials are discussing the possibility of extending the travel ban for only 90 days as opposed to the typical year-long extension. This reduced period is intended to signal to the Libyan government that Washington might be willing to upgrade relations if Libya is more forthcoming on the issues of terrorism and weapons of mass destruction.

Despite its oil wealth, the Libyan economy remains hobbled by inefficient state controls and corruption. Libya's rapid population growth has also led to rising unemployment, currently estimated at 30 percent. In addition, years of sanctions have taken a toll on the lucrative oil sector, with production down to 1.3 million barrels per day from 3.7 million barrels per day in the 1970s. Acknowledging the need for change, Qadhafi has authorized wide-ranging economic reforms. In June, the Libyan leader announced a plan to privatize the economy and promote direct foreign investment. In a bid to attract foreign investment, the exchange rate was liberalized and trade licenses were abolished to allow integration with the global market. Libya has also applied to join the World Trade Organization.

Political Rights and Civil Liberties:

Libyans cannot change their government democratically. Colonel Muammar al-Qadhafi rules by decree with little accountability or transparency. Libya's governing principles stem from Qadhafi's *Green Book*, a treatise that combines Islamic ideals with elements of socialism and pan-Arabism. Qadhafi rejects Western-style democracy and political parties, claiming instead that his country is a *jamahiriyah*, or state of the masses. As such, Qadhafi calls for direct popular rule. The reality, however, is that power is tightly held by Qadhafi and a relatively small inner circle of advisers.

Libyans do not have the right to organize into different political parties. While people do play a role in popular congresses, they do not affect the balance of power that remains squarely in Qadhafi's control. Extra-governmental bodies, including the revolutionary committees and people's committees, aid Qadhafi and serve as tools of repression. There is no significant legal opposition in Libya, and people's political choices are subject to the domination of Qadhafi and his esoteric political system.

Free media do not exist in Libya. The government severely limits freedom of speech and of the press, particularly any criticism of Qadhafi. The state owns and controls all print and broadcast media outlets and thereby maintains a monopoly on the flow of information. Satellite television is widely available, although foreign programming is censored at times. Internet access is limited, as there is only one service provider (owned by Qadhafi's son). However, reportedly, the number of Internet users is growing.

Freedom of religion is restricted, and the government controls most mosques and Islamic institutions in Libya, which is 97 percent Sunni Muslim. Islamic organizations whose teachings and beliefs differ from the official, government-approved version of Islam are banned. Academic freedom is severely restricted.

Freedom of assembly, demonstration, and open public discussion are severely restricted. Qadhafi maintains an extensive internal security apparatus. The Libyan leader is ruthless with suspected opponents and is able to mobilize his multilayered security apparatus quickly. These multiple and overlapping security services rely on an extensive network of informers that are present throughout Libyan society.

The judiciary is not independent. Security forces have the power to pass sentences without a trial, and the government has used summary judicial proceedings to suppress domestic dissent. Political trials are held in secret with no due process considerations. Arbitrary arrest and torture are commonplace. In October, Amnesty International called on the Libyan authorities to release or grant new trials to 151 students and professionals who have been detained since 1998. They were charged with belonging to an unauthorized group, the Libyan Islamic Group, and have been denied access to a fair trial since that time.

The largely Berber and Tuareg minorities face discrimination. While women's status has improved in some areas like education and employment, discrimination continues in other areas where local traditions predominate. Female genital mutilation is still practiced in remote rural areas. Violence against women also continues to be a problem.

Morocco

Population: 30,400,000 **Political Rights:** 5
GNI/capita: $1,190 **Civil Liberties:** 5
Life Expectancy: 70 **Status:** Partly Free
Religious Groups: Muslim (98.7 percent),
Christian (1.1 percent), Jewish (0.2 percent)
Ethnic Groups: Arab-Berber (99 percent),
other (1 percent)
Capital: Rabat

Ten-Year Ratings Timeline (Political Rights, Civil Liberties, Status)

1994	1995	1996	1997	1998	1999	2000	2001	2002	2003
5,5PF	5,5PF	5,5PF	5,5PF	5,4PF	5,4PF	5,4PF	5,5PF	5,5PF	5,5PF

Overview: Shaken by five simultaneous suicide bombings on May 16, 2003 that left 45 dead and nearly 100 injured, Morocco has engaged in a security crackdown that has prompted criticism from press freedom and human rights organizations. A new antiterrorism law that erodes human rights protections and increased reports of torture have raised significant concerns. Meanwhile, the Islamists are on the defensive, downplaying their political ambitions during the September 12 municipal elections. King Muhammad VI proposed significant reform of the Mudawana, Morocco's personal status code, which would grant broad new rights to women if passed by parliament.

Moroccan independence dates to 1956, when power passed to King Muhammad V following 44 years of French colonial rule. King Hassan II ascended the throne five years later on the death of his father. In 1975, Morocco laid claim to the Western Sahara following the withdrawal of Spanish forces from the territory. The status of the territory remains in dispute. Hassan II oversaw much of Morocco's modern development; however, despite Hassan's gestures at establishing a constitutional monarchy, power remained concentrated entirely in the hands of the king. The country's stability was shaken during the early 1970s, when two assassination attempts on the king were thwarted. King Hassan embarked on a slow path toward political reform in the 1990s. In 1996, the king established a directly elected lower house of parliament via a constitutional amendment. Hassan also moved to improve the human rights situation and modestly expand political freedoms.

At age 35, King Muhammad VI came to power in July 1999 after the death of his father. While Morocco had made tentative steps toward political and economic liberalization, Muhammad inherited a country with severe social and economic problems. More than 20 percent of the population was unemployed, nearly half remained illiterate, and a third lived below the poverty line. Mounting public debt impinged on the government's ability to provide social services. Islamist charitable networks quickly filled the gap, providing services and gaining support at the grassroots level.

King Muhammad has continued to pursue political opening, although at a measured pace. Soon after he ascended the throne, the young king distinguished himself through a series of bold maneuvers. One of his first acts was to dismiss Driss Basri, long considered one of the most powerful men in Morocco and, in many ways, the embodiment of corruption and repression that marked the monarchy. Thousands of prisoners were released, and the king allowed exile opposition figures to return to Morocco.

In 2002, Morocco held parliamentary elections that were widely considered to be the most representative in the country's history. While the vote did not alter the fundamental distribution of power in Morocco, the resulting diversity in parliament—with 10 percent women and a significant Islamist presence—constituted an important step toward greater political openness.

Five suicide bombings in May 2003 shattered Morocco's sense of stability. Arrests of Islamic extremists, including three Saudi members of al-Qaeda, had taken place during 2002, but the terrorist attack signaled a new and disturbing escalation in terrorist activity. Victims were primarily Moroccans, and the targets included visible symbols of Morocco's Jewish community. While Moroccan officials initially blamed foreign extremists, the 14 attackers were Moroccan and believed to be part of a local extremist group identified as As-Sirat al-Mustaqim, the Righteous Path. The group is based in the slums of Casablanca and could be responsible for a series of assassinations of "unbelievers" from the neighborhood. However, the attackers may have received external funding and training. The extremists' links to al-Qaeda remain unclear; in an audiotape purportedly made by Osama bin Laden in 2002, Morocco was listed among countries "ready for liberation."

The Moroccan government's response to the attacks has been both swift and harsh. Approximately 1,100 terrorism suspects were arrested in the ensuing crackdown. The courts have sentenced more than 50 people to life in prison and 16 people to death. Meanwhile, the Moroccan Human Rights Association has said that the trials appear to be seriously flawed. Few witnesses are called, and acquittals are rare.

Municipal elections were held on September 12; the government postponed the elections from June in the wake of the May suicide bombings. The Islamist Justice and Development Party (PJD) made a conscious decision to lower its profile and run fewer candidates in the local election. Although the PJD denounced the terrorist bombings, the party has found itself under fire in a political atmosphere that is less tolerant of Islamists. As a result, the PJD ran for only 18 percent of the council seats contested, including the Islamist stronghold of Casablanca and the key cities of Fez and Rabat. The Islamist party put up only 3 percent of all candidates. Under pressure from the government, the Islamist party opted to step down rather than risk a greater government crackdown. Yet, the two principal secular parties—the Socialist Union of Popular Forces (USFP) and the Istiqlal—failed to capitalize on the Islamists' absence, despite running candidates in nearly every jurisdiction. Neither party was able to capture the town halls of Casablanca, Marrakesh, or Tangiers.

Political Rights and Civil Liberties: Moroccans' right to change their government democratically is limited. The monarch retains ultimate authority. He may appoint or approve the government and can, at his discretion, dismiss any member of the cabinet, dissolve parliament, call for new elections, and rule by decree. Legislative powers are shared by the king and a bicameral legislature that includes a directly elected lower house. Unlike previous votes, the 2002 parliamentary elections and the 2003 municipal elections were regarded as the most representative in the country's history.

Opposition parties remain weak. The government crackdown on Islamic extremists clearly has deterred moderate Islamist elements from political participation, as witnessed by their decision to roll back dramatically their presence in the local elections. Secular opposition parties have yet to make significant inroads at the grassroots level, nor have they found common cause with the Islamists who have pushed for greater reforms.

Press freedoms remain somewhat restricted. Broadcast media are mostly government controlled and largely reflect official views, although foreign broadcasting is available via satellite. The Committee to Protect Journalists noted a disturbing trend toward censorship with the Moroccan print media. Since May, eight Moroccan journalists have been detained in connection with their work and five remain in jail. The journalists were convicted on charges of "insulting the king" and undermining the monarchy. Prison sentences range from 18 months to three years. Meanwhile, publication of two Casablanca-based satirical weeklies has been suspended. The deterioration in press freedoms appears to be a result of the government crackdown following the May bombings. An antiterrorism law passed soon after the attacks has been used repeatedly to detain reporters.

Islam is the official religion of Morocco, and almost 99 percent of the population is Sunni Muslim. Morocco's Jewish community, while quite small (approximately 5,000), has been able to worship freely. However, in 2003 a disturbing trend of attacks on the Jewish community became apparent. Aside from the May bombings, where four out of the five sites were Jewish or had Jewish connections, a Jewish merchant was assassinated in Casablanca on September 11.

Freedom of association is limited. Nongovernment organizations must receive government permission to operate legally. The Interior Ministry requires permits for public gatherings and has forcibly dispersed demonstrations in the past. However, peaceful protests are generally tolerated.

The judiciary lacks independence and is subject to corruption and bribery. Days after the May bombings, parliament adopted a tough anti-terrorism law that allows terror suspects to be held up to 12 days without being charged; the law also broadens the definition of terrorism and expands the number of crimes punishable by death. Amnesty International says the practice of torture has widened in Morocco as part of the antiterrorism campaign. Some terror suspects interviewed by Amnesty told of being held for weeks in secret detention and subject to various forms of torture. Human rights groups have also criticized the trials of terror suspects that often last only two or three days. Many suspects are convicted on the basis of their statements to police without any material proof of their guilt. Among those convicted are 14-year-old twins who were sentenced to five years in prison for plotting to blow up the liquor aisle of a supermarket.

While Moroccan women are guaranteed equal rights under the constitution, the reality in both the political and social spheres has been one of marked inequality. However, in October 2003, King Muhammad VI proposed far-reaching reforms of Morocco's personal status code. The changes include raising the marriage age from 15 to 18 for women and allowing women the right to initiate divorce. The reforms would also make polygamy quite difficult and, in general, cede greater rights to women in the areas of marriage and divorce. The reforms still need to be approved by parliament. Similar changes were proposed for the Mudawana in 2000, but met with stiff opposition from the Islamists. King Muhammad appears to be taking advantage of the Islamists' defensive posture to push through these significant reforms. Many women pursue careers in the professions or in government, but they face restrictions in advancement. Domestic violence is common, and the law is lenient toward men who kill their wives for alleged adultery.

Oman

Population: 2,600,000 **Political Rights:** 6
GNI/capita: $7,720 **Civil Liberties:** 5
Life Expectancy: 73 **Status:** Not Free
Religious Groups: Ibadi Muslim (75 percent,) other
[including Sunni Muslim, Shi'a Muslim, Hindu] (25 percent)
Ethnic Groups: Arab, Baluchi, South Asian, African
Capital: Muscat

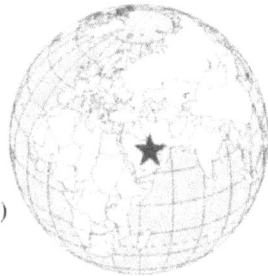

Ten-Year Ratings Timeline (Political Rights, Civil Liberties, Status)

1994	1995	1996	1997	1998	1999	2000	2001	2002	2003
6,6NF	6,6NF	6,6NF	6,6NF	6,6NF	6,6NF	6,5NF	6,5NF	6,5NF	6,5NF

Overview: Oman took a small step forward in opening up its political system in October 2003 by holding the first full election in its history, for its Consultative Council. Nevertheless, the Consultative Council, which is the lower chamber of the bicameral Council of Oman, has advisory rather than legislative powers.

Oman has been an independent nation since Sultan bin Seif's expulsion of the Portuguese in 1650, ending more than a century of Portuguese involvement in certain regions of Oman. After the expulsion of the Portuguese, the sultan conquered neighboring territories, building a small empire that included parts of the eastern coast of Africa and the southern Arabian Peninsula.

During the 1950s and 1960s, Oman experienced a period of internal unrest centered mostly on the interior regions of the country. In 1964, a group of separatists supported by Communist governments, such as the People's Democratic Republic of Yemen, or former South Yemen, started a revolt in Oman's Dhofar province. This insurgency was not completely quelled until the mid-1970s, with Oman's government receiving direct military support from its traditional ally the United Kingdom, as well as from Iran and Jordan.

The current ruler, Sultan Qaboos, came to power more than 30 years ago, after overthrowing his father, Sultan Said bin Taimur, who had ruled for nearly four decades. Sultan Qaboos launched a program to modernize Oman's infrastructure, educational system, governmental structure, and economy.

In 1991, Sultan Qaboos established the Consultative Council, or Majlis Ashshura, an appointed body aimed at providing the sultan with a wider range of opinions on ruling the country. The 1996 basic law, promulgated by a royal decree from Sultan Qaboos, transformed the Consultative Council into an elected body, but the right to vote in these elections was not granted to all citizens; only a limited number of citizens selected by tribal leaders were allowed to participate in the first elections. The basic law granted certain civil liberties, banned discrimination on the basis of sex, religion, ethnicity, and social class, and clarified the process for royal succession.

This limited political reform in the 1990s was overshadowed by a stronger effort to reform Oman's oil-dependent economy. In 1995, Sultan Qaboos spearheaded an effort to liberalize Oman's economy, reduce its dependence on oil exports, and attract international investments. In preparation for its eventual accession to the World Trade Organization (WTO) as a full member in 2000, Oman lifted restrictions on foreign investment and ownership of enterprises in the country. In 2000, Oman launched its sixth five-year plan for the economy, which places emphasis on the "Omanization" of the labor force and job creation in the private sector, and more specific focus on Oman's interior regions, which continue to lag behind the coastal regions. Today, the petroleum sector contributes about 40 percent of Oman's gross domestic product, down from 70 percent in the 1980s.

In October 2003, Oman held the first full election in its history, for its 83-member Consultative Council. Though the powers of the Consultative Council remain limited, the election marked the first time that Oman gave the right to vote to all adult citizens, both men and women. Nearly three-quarters of registered voters participated in the election, which marks another modest step in introducing political reforms.

Political Rights and Civil Liberties:

Citizens of Oman do not have the right to elect their country's leaders democratically. Citizens can express their views only in a very limited way, by electing members to the Consultative Council, which has no legislative powers and may only recommend changes to new laws. The Consultative Council is half of a bicameral body known as the Council of Oman; the other half, a 57-member State Council, is appointed by the sultan. The sultan has absolute power and issues laws by decree. Mechanisms for citizens to petition the government through local government officials exist, and certain citizens are afforded limited opportunities to petition the sultan in direct meetings. Political parties are banned by law, and no meaningful organized political opposition exists.

Freedom of expression and democratic debate is limited in Oman, with laws prohibiting criticism of the sultan. The government owns and controls all broadcast media outlets, which have the broadest reach to the Omani population. During 2003, the government allowed state television to broadcast sessions in which members of the Consultative Council questioned government ministers. As with other countries in the Arab world, the number of households with access to satellite television has increased, leading to an expansion in the diversity of sources of information.

However, this information is mostly focused on regional issues. Oman's government permits private print publications, although many of these publications accept government subsidies and practice self-censorship. Omanis have access to the Internet through the national telecommunications company, and the government censors politically sensitive and pornographic content.

Islam is the state religion, and Sharia (Islamic law) is the source of all legislation, according to the basic law. Non-Muslims have the right to worship, although non-Muslim religious organizations must register with the government. The Ministry of Awqaf (Religious Charitable Bequests) and Religious Affairs distributes standardized texts for mosque sermons and expects imams to stay within the outlines of these texts. The government restricts academic freedom by preventing the publication of politically sensitive topics.

The basic law allows the formation of nongovernmental organizations, but civic and associational life remains quite limited in Oman. All public gatherings require government permission. In March 2003, police used moderate force to disperse public demonstrations against the war in Iraq. Oman has no labor or trade unions. In April 2003, the government issued a decree that removed a previous prohibition on strikes. Complaints related to labor and working conditions are managed by the Ministry of Social Affairs and Labor and mediated by the Labor Welfare Board.

Although the basic law states that the judiciary is independent, it remains subordinate to the sultan and the Ministry of Justice. Sharia courts are responsible for family law matters such as divorce and inheritance. In less populated areas, tribal laws and customs are frequently used to adjudicate disputes. According to the law, arbitrary arrest and detention are prohibited. In practice, the police are not required to obtain an arrest warrant in advance. Many of the civil liberties guarantees expressed in the basic law have not been implemented.

Oman currently has a population of approximately 2.6 million people, less than 2 million of whom are Omani citizens. Most noncitizens are immigrant workers. Foreign workers at times have been placed in situations amounting to forced labor, according to the U.S. State Department's human rights report for 2002, released in March 2003.

Although the basic law prohibits discrimination on the basis of sex, women suffer from legal and social discrimination. Women must have the permission of a male relative to travel abroad. Women remain under-represented in political life in Oman, with only two women having won seats on the 83-member Consultative Council in the 2003 national elections.

↟ Qatar

Population: 600,000   **Political Rights:** 6
GNI/capita: $20,701   **Civil Liberties:** 6
Life Expectancy: 72   **Status:** Not Free
Religious Groups: Muslim (95 percent), other (5 percent)
Ethnic Groups: Arab (40 percent), Pakistani (18 percent),
Indian (18 percent), Iranian (10 percent), other (14 percent)
Capital: Doha
Trend Arrow: Qatar received an upward trend arrow due to progress on political reforms, including the approval of a new constitution and the first election of a woman to public office.

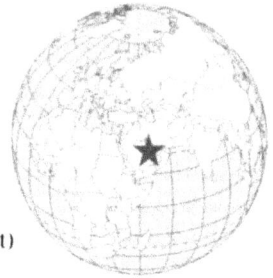

Ten-Year Ratings Timeline (Political Rights, Civil Liberties, Status)

1994	1995	1996	1997	1998	1999	2000	2001	2002	2003
7,6NF	7,6NF	7,6NF	7,6NF	7,6NF	6,6NF	6,6NF	6,6NF	6,6NF	6,6NF

Overview:
Despite concerns about regional stability resulting from the war in Iraq, Qatar took limited steps forward to introduce political reform by organizing municipal elections on April 7, 2003 and holding a national referendum on a new draft constitution on April 29. The municipal elections resulted in the first election of a woman to public office, and nearly 97 percent of the voters in the referendum approved the new constitution.

For the first half of the nineteenth century, the al-Khalifa family of Bahrain dominated the territory now known as Qatar. The Ottoman Empire occupied Qatar from 1872 until World War I, when the United Kingdom recognized Sheikh Abdullah bin Jassim al-Thani as the ruler of Qatar and Sheikh Abdullah signed a series of treaties of friendship and commerce with the United Kingdom. Following World War II, Qatar rapidly developed its oil production industry, and the oil wealth contributed to economic and social development in the country.

Qatar became formally independent in 1971. From 1971 to 1995, Emir Khalifa bin Hamad al-Thani ruled as an absolute monarch, with few government institutions checking his authority. In 1995, the emir was deposed by his son Hamad, who began a program to introduce gradual political, social, and economic reforms. Hamad dissolved the Information Ministry shortly after taking power, an action designed to demonstrate his commitment to expand press freedom.

In 1996, Hamad permitted the creation of Al-Jazeera, which has become one of the most popular Arabic language satellite television channels. Al-Jazeera, however, generally does not cover Qatari politics and focuses instead on regional issues such as the situation in Iraq and the Arab-Israeli conflict. In the past few years, Sheikh Hamad accelerated a program to build Qatar's educational institutions, attracting foreign universities to establish branches in Qatar; Cornell Medical School opened a branch in Doha in 2002. In 1999, Qatar held elections for a 29-member municipal council and became the first state of the Gulf Cooperation Council (GCC) to introduce universal suffrage.

In 2002, a 38-member committee appointed by Hamad presented a draft constitution, which was refined and presented to the public in a referendum in April 2003.

This new constitution, which was approved by almost 97 percent of voters, slightly broadens the scope of political participation without eliminating the monopoly on power enjoyed by the al-Thani family. This limited progress on political reform took place despite regional tensions over the war in Iraq: Qatar was the location of the forward headquarters for the United States Central Command.

Political Rights and Civil Liberties: Qataris do not have the power to change the top leadership in their government democratically. They possess only limited power to elect representatives who serve in local government positions, which have circumscribed powers and report to the minister of municipal affairs and agriculture, who is appointed by the emir. The head of state is the emir, and the al-Thani family controls a monopoly on political power in Qatar. The emir appoints a prime minister and the cabinet. The constitution states that the emir appoints an heir after consulting with the royal family and other notables. The new constitution, ratified by public referendum in 2003, provides for elections to 30 of the 45 seats in a new advisory council, and the government announced tentative plans to hold these elections in 2004. The government does not permit the existence of political parties.

The new constitution guarantees freedom of expression, and the state has generally refrained from direct censorship. However, content in the print and broadcast media is influenced by leading families. The five leading daily newspapers are privately owned, but their owners and board members include royal family members and other notables. Although the satellite television channel Al-Jazeera is privately owned, the Qatari government has reportedly paid operating costs for the channel since its inception. Qataris have access to the Internet through a telecommunications monopoly, which has recently been privatized, but the government censors content and blocks access to certain sites deemed pornographic or politically sensitive.

Islam is Qatar's official religion, and the new constitution explicitly provides for freedom of worship. The Ministry of Islamic Affairs regulates clerical affairs and the construction of mosques. Converting to another religion from Islam is considered apostasy and is a capital offense, but there have been no reports of executions for apostasy since 1971. Qatar's government has also begun outreach efforts to build better relations between Islam and other religions by sponsoring a dialogue on Muslim-Christian understanding and establishing diplomatic relations with the Vatican. The new constitution provides for freedom of opinion and research, but scholars often practice self-censorship on politically sensitive topics.

The constitution provides for freedom of assembly and the right to form organizations, but these rights are limited in practice. Public protests and demonstrations are rare, with the government placing strict limits on the public's ability to organize demonstrations. All nongovernmental organizations require state permission to operate, and the government closely monitors the activities of these groups. There are no independent human rights organizations, but a National Committee for Human Rights, consisting of members of civil society and government ministries, has done some work on investigating allegations of human rights abuses.

The law prohibits labor unions, but allows joint consultative committees of employers and workers to deal with disputes. Foreign national workers, who make up most of the workforce in Qatar, face severe disadvantages in labor contract cases.

Several strikes took place in 2003, including one in May by 350 employees at an engineering firm over five months of unpaid wages and a sit-in by several hundred workers in a construction company to protest a salary payment dispute.

Although the constitution guarantees that the judiciary is independent, this is not true in practice. The majority of Qatar's judges are foreign nationals who are appointed and removed by the emir. Qatar's judicial system consists of two sets of courts: Sharia (Islamic law) courts, which have jurisdiction over a narrow range of issues, such as family law; and civil courts, which have jurisdiction over commercial and civil suits. These two sets of courts have been united under the Supreme Judiciary Council. The constitution protects individuals from arbitrary arrest and detention and bans torture, and defendants are entitled to legal representation. There are no reports of widespread violations of human rights in Qatar. Prisons meet international standards, and the police generally follow proper procedures set in accordance with the law.

Women have the right to participate in elections and run for elective office. In the April 2003 municipal elections, Sheikha Yousef Hassan al-Jufairi became the first woman elected to public office. However, legally and socially, women face discrimination. For example, women must have permission from a male guardian to obtain a driver's license or travel abroad.

Saudi Arabia

Population: 24,100,000   **Political Rights:** 7
GNI/capita: $8,460   **Civil Liberties:** 7
Life Expectancy: 72   **Status:** Not Free
Religious Groups: Muslim (100 percent)
Ethnic Groups: Arab (90 percent), Afro-Asian (10 percent)
Capital: Riyadh

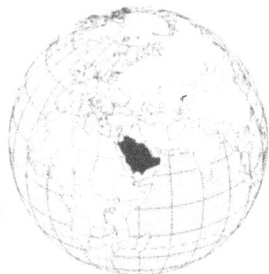

Ten-Year Ratings Timeline (Political Rights, Civil Liberties, Status)

1994	1995	1996	1997	1998	1999	2000	2001	2002	2003
7,7NF	7,7NF	7,7NF	7,7NF	7,7NF	7,7NF	7,7NF	7,7NF	7,7NF	7,7NF

Overview: Saudi Arabia continued to place severe restrictions on its citizens' political rights and civil liberties in 2003, even as hints of possible political reforms emerged in an eventful year for the kingdom. Throughout the year, the country faced threats to its internal stability from terrorist groups and calls for political reform from dissidents and regime opponents. The government of Saudi Arabia responded by offering several signs of possible limited political reforms: the approval of the formation of the first Saudi human rights organization, the first official sanction of a human rights conference in the kingdom, the establishment of a center for dialogue on reform, and announcements of local elections to be held next year.

In the 71 years since its unification in 1932 by King Abdul Aziz Al-Saud, Saudi Arabia has been controlled by the Al-Saud family, with King Fahd, the current king, the fifth in the Al-Saud ruling dynasty. The Saudi monarchy rules in accordance with the conservative school of Sunni Islam. In the early 1990s, Fahd embarked on a limited program of political reform, introducing an appointed consultative council, or Majlis Ash-shura. This step did not lead to any substantial shift in political power. In 1995, King Fahd suffered a stroke, and since 1997, Crown Prince Abdullah has taken control of most power and decision making.

With the largest oil reserves in the world, Saudi Arabia is the world's leading oil producer and exporter. Saudi Arabia's oil wealth and importance to the global economy are key features impacting the country's external relations and shaping Saudi Arabia's internal politics by giving the Al-Saud dynasty unmatched wealth to maintain its control.

Saudi Arabia has been under intense scrutiny since the September 11, 2001 attacks against the United States—15 of the 19 hijackers were Saudi citizens, and the leader of al-Qaeda, Osama bin Ladin, is from a wealthy Saudi family. In 2003, the Saudi monarchy took some first steps to stop the flow of financial support to terrorist groups, agreeing for the first time to set up a joint task force with the United States to target suspected terrorist financiers. The government passed the country's first anti–money laundering law, making financing of terrorist organizations a punishable offense. Saudi Arabia banned all charities from sending money abroad without official approval, audited hundreds of domestic organizations, and closed dozens of charities for suspected involvement in terrorist financing. Saudi Crown Prince Abdullah traveled to Russia in the first high-level Saudi visit to Moscow in 75 years to discuss measures to cut off Saudi financing of separatists in Chechnya.

The threat of terrorist attacks has also posed a challenge to the stability of the Saudi regime. A triple suicide bombing that killed 35 people in Riyadh on May 12, 2003 was a wake-up call for the Saudi monarchy, leading to a crackdown that included the interrogation of thousands of Saudi citizens. In early November, another suicide attack left 18 more Saudis dead. The government fired numerous clerics for inciting hatred and preaching an intolerant version of Islam. The Saudi Interior Ministry, fearing that children might have been recruited by militants, made a public appeal to families to report any missing children.

The Saudi government's dominance of the economy, endemic corruption, and financial mismanagement has led to mounting economic woes, with the world's largest oil producer seeing a decline in real GDP per person over the last decade. Unemployment is estimated at 30 percent, and this year, the Saudi government recognized the growing problem of poverty by announcing a strategy to create jobs and build housing for the underprivileged.

Amid these growing economic difficulties and increased access to outside sources of information through satellite television and the Internet, pressure for political change has mounted. Foreign Minister Prince Saud Al-Faisal announced this year a royal decree approving the establishment of Saudi Arabia's first nongovernmental human rights organization. During the summer, Saudi Arabia established the King Abdul Aziz Center for National Dialogue, which is aimed at starting internal discussions on political reform. In September, more than 300 prominent professionals, including 51 women, sent a petition to Crown Prince Abdullah demanding an elected legislature to replace the appointed consultative council, an independent judiciary, and the creation of civil society organizations to promote greater tolerance.

In October, Saudi Arabia organized the country's first human rights conference, a three-day event that examined human rights in an Islamic context. The conference, however, focused on double standards in Western countries rather than the massive human rights abuse problems within the kingdom. During this conference, protestors demanding political reform took to the streets, inspired by the Movement for Islamic Reform in Arabia, a London-based group of Saudi dissidents who set up the first opposition broadcasting network in Saudi Arabia.

In the face of these demands to make its government more open and accessible, Saudi Arabia announced plans to hold local elections in 2004. In November, the Saudi regime said it would start televising 30-minute excerpts of weekly sessions of the Shura Council. Time will tell if these limited reform measures are the start of something broader and more consequential.

Political Rights and Civil Liberties:

Saudi Arabia is an absolute monarchy, and its citizens have no power to change the government democratically. The country's 1992 Basic Law declares that the Quran is the country's constitution. Saudi Arabia has a 120-member consultative Shura Council appointed by the monarch, but this council has limited powers and does not impact decision making or power structures in a meaningful way.

The country has never held elections for public office at any level. On October 13, 2003, the Saudi government announced it would hold its first elections to select half of the members of municipal councils in parts of the country in 2004. However, the government released few details about these planned elections, and several questions remained, such as whether or not women would be allowed to participate.

Saudi Arabia does not have political parties, and the only semblance of organized political opposition exists outside of the country. Many Saudi opposition activists are based in London. The Al-Saud dynasty dominates and controls political life in the kingdom.

The Council of Ministers, an executive body appointed by the king, passes legislation that becomes law once ratified by royal decree. The Saudi monarchy has a tradition of consulting with select members of Saudi society, but this process is not equally open to all citizens. Corruption is one consequence of the closed nature of Saudi Arabia's government and society, with foreign companies reporting that they often pay bribes to middle men and government officials to secure business deals.

Government authorities frequently ban or fire journalists and editors who publish articles deemed offensive to the country's powerful religious establishment or the ruling authorities. This year, Hussein Shabakshi, a journalist who advocated for elections, human rights, and women's equality in one of his weekly columns in the Saudi daily *Okaz*, was banned by the Saudi Ministry of Interior. Jamal Khasshogi, editor of the reformist newspaper *Al-Watan*, was fired for writing articles critical of the religious establishment.

Religious freedom does not exist in Saudi Arabia, the birthplace of Islam and the location of the two holiest cities of Islam, Mecca and Medina. Islam is Saudi Arabia's official religion, and all citizens are required by law to be Muslims. The government prohibits the public practice of any religions other than Islam. Although the government recognizes the right of non-Muslims to worship in private, it does not always respect this right in practice. Academic freedom is restricted in Saudi Arabia, and informers monitor classrooms for compliance with limits on curriculums, such as a ban on teaching Western philosophy and religions other than Islam.

Saudi citizens do not have any associational or organizational rights, and there is no freedom to form political organizations or to hold protests. In October, Saudi security officials detained hundreds of protestors calling for political reform. Trade unions, collective bargaining, and strikes are prohibited.

The judiciary lacks independence from the monarchy. The king appoints all judges on the recommendation of the Supreme Judicial Council, and the monarchy serves as the highest court of appeal. The rule of law is regularly flouted by the Saudi regime, with frequent trials falling short of international standards. Secret trials are common, and political opponents of the Saudi regime are often detained without charge and held for indefinite periods of time. Allegations of torture by police and prison officials are frequent, though access to prisoners by independent human rights and legal organizations is strictly limited.

Although racial discrimination is illegal according to Saudi law, substantial prejudice against ethnic, religious, and national minorities exists. Foreign workers from Asia and Africa are subject to formal and informal discrimination and have difficulty obtaining justice.

Citizens have the right to own property and establish private businesses, but much private enterprise activity is connected with members of the ruling family and the government. Although Saudi Arabia first joined the General Agreement on Tariffs and Trade in 1993, its slow process of privatization and economic reform has prevented it from becoming a member of the World Trade Organization (WTO). In the past year, Saudi Arabia has taken steps to diversify its economic structures and establish government regulatory organizations to strengthen its market economy. The Saudi government passed a new foreign investment law that would ease restrictions on investment and announced plans to cut tax rates and custom duties. As a result, WTO head Supachai Panitchpakdi announced in 2003 that Saudi Arabia would likely be invited to join the WTO in early 2004.

Women are not treated as equal members of Saudi Arabian society. Women legally may not drive cars, and their use of public facilities is restricted when men are present. By law and custom, women cannot travel within or outside of the country without a male relative. Saudi laws discriminate against women in a range of matters including family law, and a woman's testimony is treated as inferior to a man's in court. The Committee to Prevent Vice and Promote Virtue, a semiautonomous religious police force commonly known as the *mutawa'een*, enforce a strict policy of segregation between men and women and oftentimes use physical punishment to ensure that women meet conservative standards of dress in public.

Syria

Population: 17,500,000   **Political Rights:** 7
GNi/capita: $1,040   **Civil Liberties:** 7
Life Expectancy: 70   **Status:** Not Free
Religious Groups: Sunni Muslim (74 percent), other
Muslim [including Alawite and Druze] (16 percent),
Christian [various sects] (10 percent)
Ethnic Groups: Arab (90 percent), other, [including Kurd
and Armenian] (10 percent)
Capital: Damascus

Ten-Year Ratings Timeline (Political Rights, Civil Liberties, Status)

1994	1995	1996	1997	1998	1999	2000	2001	2002	2003
7,7NF	7,7NF	7,7NF	7,7NF	7,7NF	7,7NF	7,7NF	7,7NF	7,7NF	7,7NF

Overview: In the face of growing international pressure to end his government's sponsorship of militant terrorist groups and the fall of a sister Baathist government in neighboring Iraq, Syrian President Bashar Assad came under mounting domestic pressure in 2003 to reform the repressive and corrupt political system built by his father. Although some nominal political and economic reforms were introduced, government suppression of political and civil liberties continued, with dozens of people arrested during the year for peacefully expressing their opinions.

Located at the heart of the Fertile Crescent, the Syrian capital of Damascus is the oldest continuously inhabited city in the world and once controlled a vast empire extending from Europe to India. The modern state of Syria is a comparatively recent entity, established by the French after World War I and formally granted independence in 1946. The pan-Arab Baath Party, which seized control of Syria 40 years ago, has long sought to extend its writ beyond Syrian borders. For all its pan-Arab pretensions, however, the Syrian government has been dominated by Alawites, adherents of an offshoot sect of Islam who constitute just 12 percent of the population, since a 1970 coup brought Gen. Hafez Assad to power. For the next 30 years, the Assad regime managed to maintain control of the majority Sunni Muslim population only by brutally suppressing all dissent. In 1982, government forces stormed the northern town of Hama to crush a rebellion by the Muslim Brotherhood and killed as many as 20,000 insurgents and civilians in a matter of days.

In 2000, Assad's son and successor, Bashar, inherited control of a country with one of the most stagnant economies and highest rates of population growth in the region, with unemployment estimated at more than 20 percent. In his inaugural speech, the young Syrian leader pledged to eliminate government corruption, revitalize the economy, and establish a "democracy specific to Syria, which takes its roots from its history and respects its society."

The first six months of Assad's tenure brought dramatic changes. Loose networks of public figures from all sectors of civil society were allowed to discuss the country's social, economic, and political problems in informal gatherings. Assad released more than 600 political prisoners, closed the notorious Mazzeh prison, allowed scores of exiled dissidents to return home, reinstated dissidents who had been fired from state-run media outlets and universities, and instructed the state-run media to give a voice to reformers. The "Damascus Spring" reached its zenith in January 2001 with the establishment of the country's first privately owned newspaper.

In February 2001, however, the regime abruptly reimposed restrictions on public freedoms and launched an escalating campaign of threats, intimidation, and harassment against the reform movement. By the end of the year, ten leading reformists had been arrested. In 2002, the "Damascus Ten" were sentenced to prison terms, while the security agencies arrested over a dozen additional journalists, human rights activists, and political dissidents. The regime's renewed assault on political and civil liberties initially elicited little criticism from Western governments, in part because of Assad's cooperation in the war against al-Qaeda. Economic reform also fell by the wayside as dozens of reform laws remained unimplemented or were put into effect half-heartedly; hopes for a much-needed influx of foreign investment faded.

The March 2003 U.S.-led invasion of Iraq, a country hitherto ruled by a rival branch of the Baath Party, posed serious problems for the Assad regime. The downfall of Saddam Hussein brought an end to Iraqi shipments of cut-rate petroleum supplies, which had helped the government weather dismal economic conditions without implementing major reforms. Scenes of Iraqis celebrating the downfall of a regime so similar to the one in Damascus inspired Syria's pro-democracy movement to reassert itself. In late May, nearly 300 intellectuals signed a petition demanding the release of all political prisoners, the cancellation of the state of emergency, and other political reforms.

After the fall of Baghdad, the Syrian government introduced a number of largely cosmetic social and political reforms. The requirement that Syrian school children wear military-style khaki uniforms was lifted, and the ministry of education was given the authority to make decisions without prior approval from the Baath Party's education bureau. In June, the government decreed that Baath Party membership would no longer affect advancement in the civil service. On the economic front, Assad eased laws on foreign currency transactions, approved the establishment of the country's first private banks and universities, and announced plans to set up a stock market. In September, Assad appointed a new prime minister and cabinet ostensibly committed to economic reform.

Syrian relations with the United States rapidly deteriorated during the invasion of Iraq, when U.S. officials publicly accused Damascus of shipping weapons to the Iraqi military and sending "volunteers" across the border to fight coalition forces. The Bush administration also intensified its calls for Syria to stop sponsoring terrorist groups opposed to the Israeli-Palestinian peace process and abandon its weapons of mass destruction (WMD) programs. In October, the Bush administration publicly endorsed an Israeli air strike on an alleged terrorist training camp outside of Damascus and announced its support for congressional sanctions on Syria.

Political Rights and Civil Liberties: The Assad regime wields absolute authority in Syria and Syrians cannot change their government through democratic means. Under the 1973 constitution, the president is nominated by the ruling Baath Party and approved by a popular referendum. In practice, these referendums are orchestrated by the regime, as are elections to the 250-

member People's Assembly, which holds little independent legislative power. The only legal political parties are the Baath Party and six small parties that comprise the ruling National Progressive Front (NPF).

Parliamentary elections in March 2003 were boycotted by five major opposition groups. All 167 of the NPF's candidates were elected, with "independent" candidates taking the remaining 83 seats. At least two people were arrested by the authorities for distributing pamphlets calling for a boycott.

Freedom of expression is heavily restricted. Vaguely worded articles of the Penal Code and Emergency Law give the government considerable discretion in punishing those who express dissent. The Penal Code prohibits the publication of information that opposes "the goals of the revolution," incites sectarianism, or "prevents authorities from executing their responsibilities." The broadcast media are entirely state owned, apart from a handful of non-news radio stations licensed in 2003. While there are some privately owned newspapers and magazines, a new press law enacted in September 2001 permits the government to arbitrarily deny or revoke publishing licenses for reasons "related to the public interest," and compels privately owned print media outlets to submit all material to government censors on the day of publication. Syrians are permitted to access the Internet only through state-run servers, which block access to a wide range of Web sites. Satellite dishes are illegal, but generally tolerated. In July 2003, the government revoked the publishing license of the country's leading independent newspaper, *Al-Doumari*. In May, the authorities released the Damascus bureau chief of the London-based Arabic daily *Al-Hayat*, Ibrahim Humaydi, who had been arrested in December 2002 on charges of "publishing false information."

Although the constitution requires that the president be a Muslim, there is no state religion in Syria and freedom of worship is generally respected. The Alawite minority dominates the officer corps of the military and security forces. Since the eruption of an Islamist rebellion in the late 1970s, the government has tightly monitored mosques and controlled the appointment of Muslim clergy. Academic freedom is heavily restricted. University professors have been routinely dismissed from state universities in recent years due to their involvement in the pro-democracy movement, and some have been imprisoned.

Freedom of assembly is largely nonexistent. While citizens can ostensibly hold demonstrations with prior permission from the Interior Ministry, in practice only the government, the Baath Party, or groups linked to them are allowed to organize demonstrations. In May 2003, according to the London-based Syrian Human Rights Committee, 11 people in Daraya, a suburb of Damascus, were arrested after they demonstrated against local corruption. All 11 were subsequently sentenced by the Supreme State Security Court (SSSC) to prison sentences ranging from three to four years. At least eight Kurdish activists who participated in a peaceful protest outside the Damascus headquarters of UNICEF in June were arrested and remained in prison at year's end.

Freedom of association is restricted. All nongovernmental organizations must register with the government, which generally denies registration to reformist groups. Three unregistered human rights groups have been allowed to operate in Syria, though individual members of the groups have been jailed for human rights related activities. In July 2003, Assad issued a presidential pardon for four members of the Syrian Human Rights Association arrested in 2002.

All unions must belong to the General Federation of Trade Unions (GFTU). Although ostensibly independent, the GFTU is headed by a member of the ruling Baath Party and is used by the government to control all aspects of union activity in Syria. While strikes in non-agricultural sectors are legal, they rarely occur.

While regular criminal and civil courts operate with some independence and generally safeguard defendants' rights, most politically sensitive cases are tried by two exceptional courts established under emergency law: the SSSC and the Economic Security Court (ESC). Both courts deny or limit the right to appeal, limit access to legal counsel, try most cases behind closed doors, and admit as evidence confessions obtained through torture. Abdel Rahman Shagouri was arrested in February 2003 for distributing an e-mail newsletter from a banned Web site and remained in detention throughout the year awaiting trial before the SSSC. Fourteen people were arrested in August for attending a lecture about the state of emergency in Syria and charged by the SSSC with inciting "factional conflict." A July 2003 decree reportedly stipulated that economic crimes previously tried by the ESC will henceforth be tried by criminal courts, but it is not clear whether the ESC has been abolished.

The state of emergency in force since 1963 gives the security agencies virtually unlimited authority to arrest suspects and hold them incommunicado for prolonged periods without charge. Many of the several hundred remaining political prisoners in Syria have never been tried for any offense. The security agencies, which operate independently of the judiciary, routinely extract confessions by torturing suspects and detaining members of their families. Government surveillance of dissidents is widespread. At least seven opposition figures who returned from exile in Iraq in 2003 were arrested and detained on their arrival in Syria, as were at least four exiles returning from other countries. Most were released within a few weeks, but a few reportedly remained in detention at year's end. One Syrian opposition figure who remained in Iraq, Riad al-Shouqfeh, narrowly escaped assassination on July 23. There were many reports of torture by the security forces during the year. In November, Maher Arar, a Syrian-born Canadian citizen released after ten months of detention by the authorities, publicly described the torture he experienced in captivity. According to Amnesty International, Kurdish activist Khalil Mustafa died two days after his arrest on August 8 as a result of torture.

The Kurdish minority in Syria faces cultural and linguistic restrictions, and suspected Kurdish activists are routinely dismissed from schools and jobs. Some 200,000 Syrian Kurds are deprived of citizenship and unable to obtain passports, identity cards, or birth certificates, which in turn prevents them from owning land, obtaining government employment, or voting. The September 2001 press law requires that owners and editors in chief of publications be Arabs. At least thirteen suspected Kurdish activists were arrested and jailed in 2003. Two Kurdish organizers of a December 2002 demonstration against government discrimination were put on trial before the SSSC in late 2003 on charges of advocating Kurdish secession, but no ruling had been issued by year's end.

Although most Syrians do not face travel restrictions, relatives of exiled dissidents are routinely prevented from traveling abroad and many Kurds lack the requisite documents to leave the country. Equality of opportunity has been compromised by rampant corruption and conscious government efforts to weaken the predominantly Sunni urban bourgeoisie.

The government has promoted gender equality by appointing women to senior positions in all branches of government and providing equal access to education, but many discriminatory laws remain in force. A husband may request that the Interior Ministry block his wife from traveling abroad, and women are generally barred from leaving the country with their children unless they can prove that the father has granted permission. Syrian law stipulates that an accused rapist can be acquitted if he marries his victim, and it provides for reduced sentences in cases of "honor crimes" committed by men against female relatives for alleged sexual misconduct. Personal status law for Muslim women is governed by Sharia (Islamic law) and is discriminatory in marriage, divorce, and inheritance matters. Violence against women is widespread, particularly in rural areas.

Tunisia

Population: 9,900,000   **Political Rights:** 6
GNI/capita: $2,070   **Civil Liberties:** 5
Life Expectancy: 73   **Status:** Not Free
Religious Groups: Muslim (98 percent),
Christian (1 percent), Jewish (1 percent)
Ethnic Groups: Arab (98 percent), other (2 percent)
Capital: Tunis

Ten-Year Ratings Timeline (Political Rights, Civil Liberties, Status)

1994	1995	1996	1997	1998	1999	2000	2001	2002	2003
6,5NF	6,5NF	6,5NF	6,5NF	6,5NF	6,5NF	6,5NF	6,5NF	6,5NF	6,5NF

Overview: The Tunisian government continued its repressive practices against suspected opposition figures during 2003. In its first report on Tunisia in more than a decade, Amnesty International accused the Tunisian government of systematic human rights abuses, including the arbitrary arrest and torture of suspected government opponents. President Zine el-Abidine Ben Ali announced his intention to seek an unprecedented fourth term in office.

Nationalist pressures for Tunisian independence began in the 1930s under the leadership of Habib Bourguiba, leader of the Neo-Doustour party. Bourguiba became the country's first president when Tunisia gained independence in 1956 after more than 70 years as a French protectorate. Bourguiba's vision for Tunisia led to significant initiatives in the areas of social and economic development, including the promotion of one of the most liberal personal status codes in the Arab world that ceded significant rights to women and remains unmatched in the Arab world today. He also furthered education and spending on economic development projects. However, political rights and civil liberties were severely restricted under Bourguiba's rule.

In 1987, President Ben Ali, formerly the minister of the interior, led a bloodless coup, deposing the aging Bourguiba and promising to open the political system. After an initial period of minor political reform, Ben Ali cracked down harshly on the Islamist opposition. Over time, the government's repressive practices extended beyond the Islamist opposition, with hundreds of dissidents having been jailed over the last 15 years for peacefully exercising their civil liberties.

The government's tolerance for dissent continued to diminish in 2003, which saw the continuation of widespread and systematic government abuse of human rights. Amnesty International issued a 40-page report that chronicled Tunisia's "cycle of injustice" and that pointed out a disturbing discrepancy between laws and practice. According to the report, government opponents—or anyone critical of the government—are subjected to arbitrary arrest, incommunicado detention (without access to a lawyer or family), torture, and imprisonment. While certain changes in Tunisian law provide more human rights guarantees, other legal changes, including a vague definition of "terrorism," undermine basic human rights. In other cases, rights have improved in law, but are widely violated in practice.

In July, Ben Ali—who won the last election in 1999 with 99.4 percent of the vote—announced plans to seek an unprecedented fourth 5-year term in office in 2004. A constitutional referendum last year removed the three-term limit on the presidency, paving the way for Ben Ali's decision. The referendum also raised to 75 the maximum age to become president, which means that Ben Ali will be eligible to stand again for office in 2009. Under this scenario, Ben Ali could be president until 2014.

Political Rights and Civil Liberties:

Tunisians cannot change their government democratically. The 1959 constitution accords the president significant powers, including the right to select the prime minister and cabinet, to rule by decree when the legislature is not in session, and to appoint the governors of Tunisia's 23 provinces. The legislature, by contrast, serves as a rubber stamp for the president's policies and does not provide a check on executive power. Presidential elections lack any pretense of competition. Although parliamentary elections are contrived to allow for the appearance of a multiparty legislature, the ruling Constitutional Democratic Rally (RCD) holds 148 of the 182 seats. Opposition parties play a symbolic role at best. The authorities have used "security concerns" as a pretext for repression of political dissent and critical discourse across the political spectrum.

Tunisia's press freedoms are among the most restricted in the Arab world. The government controls domestic broadcasting, as well as the circulation of both domestic and foreign publications. In addition, the government uses newsprint subsidies and control over public advertising revenues as a means for indirect censorship. Since President Zine el-Abidine Ben Ali's ascent to power, Tunisian journalists who are critical of the regime have been harassed, threatened, imprisoned, physically attacked, and censored. Two Tunisian journalists, Zouhair Yahyaoui and Hamadi Jebali, are currently in prison. Internet access is tightly controlled, and the government will at times intervene to block access to opposition Web sites.

While Islam is the state religion, the government allows for the free practice of all religions as long as it does not disturb the public order. The government controls and subsidizes mosques and pays the salaries of prayer leaders. The 1988 law on mosques stipulates that only those appointed by the government may lead activities in the mosques, which are required to remain closed except during prayer times. Academic freedom is severely restricted.

Freedom of association and assembly are sharply curtailed. After one opposition party, the Democratic Forum for Labor and Freedom, was legalized last year—eight years after its formation—the number of authorized political parties in the country increased to seven. However, several parties continue to be denied authorization. In addition, a number of politically oriented nongovernmental organizations remain unauthorized. For example, the founders of two organizations—the Tunisian Center for the Independence of the Judiciary and the International Association for the Support of Political Prisoners—have repeatedly faced obstructions in trying to become legally established. The government refuses to legalize most independent human rights organizations; their property has been subjected to vandalism and their offices to suspicious break-ins.

Human rights defenders, particularly lawyers, have been subjected to increased government harassment, including physical beatings. In August, a disabled former political prisoner was beaten on a Tunis street by four men in plainclothes; he had previously been assaulted twice in a similar fashion by state security officers. Another former political prisoner received a nine-month sentence on politically motivated charges. Both men had been helpful to international human rights organizations conducting research on Tunisia. Dissidents are frequently subjected to heavy police surveillance, travel bans, dismissals from work, interruptions in phone service, and harassment of family members. In October, Radhia Nasraoui, a leading human rights activist, initiated a hunger strike to protest systematic government harassment, beatings, and police surveillance.

There is no independent judiciary in Tunisia, with the government having used the courts to convict and imprison critics. Amnesty International has documented a pattern of executive interference in the administration of justice. At all stages of criminal proceedings, guarantees for a free trial under Tunisian and international law are disregarded. Defendants' files at times are confiscated or tampered with at trials, and political prisoners are subjected to harsh prison conditions, including solitary confinement. Arbitrary arrests and incommunicado detention occur with frequency, and torture is often used to coerce confessions. Numerous political trials failed to comply with international standards for a fair trial.

Women enjoy substantial rights, and the government has worked to advance women's rights in the areas of property ownership and support to divorced women. However, inheritance law still discriminates against women. Unlike in many countries in the Arab world, citizenship rights to a child are conveyed through either the mother or the father.

United Arab Emirates

Population: 3,900,000
GNI/capita: $19,750
Life Expectancy: 74
Religious Groups: Muslim [Shi'a (16 percent)]
(96 percent), other (4 percent)
Ethnic Groups: Arab and Iranian (42 percent), other
[including South Asian, European, and East Asian]
(58 percent)
Capital: Abu Dhabi

Political Rights: 6
Civil Liberties: 6*
Status: Not Free

Ratings Change: The United Arab Emirates' civil liberties rating declined from 5 to 6 due to a technical reevaluation of the state of personal autonomy and equality of opportunity.

Ten-Year Ratings Timeline (Political Rights, Civil Liberties, Status)

1994	1995	1996	1997	1998	1999	2000	2001	2002	2003
6,5NF	6,5NF	6,5NF	6,5NF	6,5NF	6,5NF	6,5NF	6,5NF	6,5NF	6,6NF

Overview:

The United Arab Emirates (UAE) took no major steps in improving its poor political rights and civil liberties record in 2003. Political discourse was focused on regional issues, particularly the war in Iraq, with a few protests breaking out in opposition to the war.

For most of its history, the territory of the UAE—a federation of seven separate emirates formerly known as the Trucial States—was controlled by various competing tribal forces. Attacks on shipping in waters off the coast of the UAE led British forces to conduct raids against the tribes in the nineteenth century. In 1853, the tribal leaders signed a treaty with the United Kingdom agreeing to a truce, which led to a decline in the raids on shipping. Though never formal British colonies, the territories of the UAE were provided protection by the British, and tribal leaders of the emirates often referred their disputes to the United Kingdom for mediation.

In 1971, the United Kingdom announced that it was ending its treaty relationships with the seven emirates of the Trucial States, as well as Bahrain and Qatar. Six of the seven states entered into a federation called the United Arab Emirates, and Ras al-Khaimah, the seventh state, joined in 1972. The 1971 provisional constitution kept significant power in the hands of each individual emirate.

In contrast to many of its neighbors, the UAE has achieved some success in diversifying its economy beyond dependency on the petroleum sector, building a leading free trade zone in Dubai and a major manufacturing center in Sharjah, as well as investing resources to develop its profile as a leading center for tourism in the region. In 2001, the government cracked down on corruption with arrests of senior officials. In the wake of the September 11, 2001 attacks on the World Trade Center and Pentagon, the government introduced reforms in its financial services and banking sectors to cut down on terrorist financing.

Economic reform has not been matched by political reform in the UAE, which has a closed political system in which the views of citizens are not taken into account. Recent reforms undertaken in the governance sector are generally more closely related to issues of trade, commerce, and the economy than to the enhancement of political rights and civil liberties. Political power remains in the hands of traditional tribal leaders. Shaikh Zayed bin Sultan Al-Nahyan, the current president, has ruled since the UAE was founded.

The year 2003 did not see any important events and major changes in the UAE's record on political rights and civil liberties. In March, the government did not interfere with protests against the Iraq war that took place in several locations around the country.

Political Rights and Civil Liberties:

Citizens cannot change their government democratically. The UAE has never held an election. All decisions about political leadership rest in the hands of the dynastic rulers of the seven separate emirates of the UAE. These seven leaders select a president and vice president, and the president appoints a prime minister and cabinet. The UAE has a 40-member Federal National Council with delegates appointed by the seven leaders every two years. However, the council serves only as an advisory body, reviewing proposed laws and questioning federal government ministers.

The UAE does not have political parties. Rather, the allocation of positions in the government is largely determined by tribal loyalties and economic power. Abu Dhabi, the major oil producer in the UAE, has controlled the presidency of the UAE since its inception. Citizens have limited opportunities to express their interests through traditional consultative sessions.

Although the UAE's constitution provides for freedom of expression, in practice the government severely restricts this right. Laws prohibit criticism of the government, ruling families, and friendly governments, and they also include vague provisions against statements that threaten society. As a consequence, journalists commonly practice self-censorship, and the leading media outlets in the UAE frequently publish government statements without criticism or comment. However, Dubai has a "Media Free Zone" where few restrictions on print and broadcast media produced for audiences outside of the UAE have been reported.

The UAE's constitution provides for freedom of religion. Islam is the official religion, and the majority of citizens are Sunnis. The government controls content in nearly all Sunni mosques. Shia minorities are free to worship without interference. Academic freedom is limited, with the Ministry of Education censoring textbooks and curriculums in both public and private schools. In addition, the government banned six university professors in 2002 from lecturing at the university because of their political views.

The government places limits on freedom of assembly and association. Small discussions on politics in private homes are generally tolerated, but there are limits on citizens' ability to organize broader gatherings. Public meetings require government permits. In March, the government did not interfere in protests in Al Ain, Dubai, and Ras Al-Khaimah against the Iraq war.

All nongovernmental organizations (NGOs) must register with the UAE's Ministry of Labor and Social Affairs, and registered NGOs reportedly receive subsidies from the government. In August, the government closed the Zayed Center for Coordination and Follow-up, a think tank, for publishing anti-Jewish literature and allowing anti-Semitic language on its Web site. The government explained that the closure was necessary, saying that the think tank's activities contradicted the principles of interfaith tolerance.

The UAE has no labor unions, although the government has mediated labor disputes. Foreign nations, who make up the vast majority of the UAE's workforce, are generally not offered labor protections. In July, the government issued a ban on a long-standing practice of employers forcing foreign employees to surrender their passports as a condition of employment.

The judiciary is not independent, with court rulings subject to review by the UAE's political leadership. An estimated 40 to 45 percent of judges in the court system are noncitizen foreign nationals. The constitution bans torture. However, Sharia (Islamic law) courts sometimes impose flogging sentences for individuals found guilty of drug use, prostitution, and adultery. In 2002, the Dubai police established a Human Rights Department to rehabilitate prisoners, monitor prison conditions, and conduct programs for crime victims.

The constitution provides for equality before the law. In practice, women's social, economic, and legal rights are not always protected because of incomplete implementation of the law and traditional biases against women. Women are underrepresented in government, although there are small signs of limited openings for women, with women receiving appointments at various levels of government in 2003.

Yemen

Population: 19,400,000 **Political Rights:** 5*
GNI/capita: $450 **Civil Liberties:** 5
Life Expectancy: 60 **Status:** Partly Free
Religious Groups: Muslim [including Sunni and Shi'a], other
Ethnic Groups: Arab [majority], Afro-Arab, South Asian
Capital: Sanaa
Ratings Change: Yemen's political rights rating improved from 6 to 5, and its status from Not Free to Partly Free, due to the holding of parliamentary elections that were legitimate but flawed.

Ten-Year Ratings Timeline (Political Rights, Civil Liberties, Status)

1994	1995	1996	1997	1998	1999	2000	2001	2002	2003
5,6NF	5,6NF	5,6NF	5,6NF	5,6NF	5,6NF	5,6NF	6,6NF	6,5NF	5,5PF

Overview: Yemen took a small step forward in improving the mechanisms and structures for continuing its transition to democracy in 2003 by holding parliamentary elections. However, the ruling party's lack of confidence in its own ability to compete in a fully democratic system impeded more substantial progress. The status of detainees held incommunicado remained an issue of concern during the year.

As part of the ancient Minaean, Sabaean, and Himyarite kingdoms, Yemen has a long history stretching back nearly three thousand years. For centuries, a series of imams controlled most of northern Yemen and parts of southern Yemen. The Ottoman Empire ruled many of the cities from the sixteenth to the nineteenth century, and the British Empire controlled areas in the southern part of the country in the first part of the twentieth century, including the port of Aden. Yemen was divided into two countries, the Yemen Arab Republic of the north and the People's Republic of South Yemen, which ultimately unified in 1990 after decades of conflict and tensions.

In the face of widespread poverty and illiteracy, tribal influences that limit the central government's authority in certain parts of the country, a heavily armed citizenry, and the threat of radical Islamist terrorism, Yemen has managed to take some limited steps to improve its record on political rights and civil liberties in the 13 years since its unification.

In 1999, President Ali Abdullah Saleh won a five-year term in the country's first nationwide direct presidential election, gaining 96.3 percent of the vote. Saleh's only opponent came from within the ruling General People's Congress (GPC), and his term in office was extended from five to seven years in a 2001 referendum.

Yemen's April 2003 parliamentary election, its third in the last decade, took place despite concerns that popular unrest resulting from the war in Iraq might lead to a postponement. International election observers noted that Yemen had made substantial improvements in electoral management and administration. On the surface, the elections were competitive with the opposition Islah Party taking seats in constituencies that were former strongholds of the ruling party. However, there were numerous problems with the election. Voter registration was characterized by widespread fraud and cheating, and underage voting was a widespread problem. Rather than opening the door for increased political pluralism, Yemen's parliamentary election was a missed opportunity, marred by cheating on the part of all major political parties and by reports of intimidation, use of state resources, and control of certain media outlets by the ruling party.

In addition to the parliamentary elections, another leading story in Yemen in 2003 was the continued incommunicado detention of individuals suspected of having ties to Islamic extremist groups such as al-Qaeda. Authorities in the government estimated the number of detainees at 200 to 300 individuals. The minister of the interior told parliament that a number of these individuals had been released because they had changed their views, while others remained in detention because they still held on to their militant views. Some of the releases were part of an Islamically oriented approach to rehabilitation, begun when President Saleh asked Judge Hamood Al-Hitar to form a "Dialogue Committee" to persuade fundamentalists to renounce violence and their fanatical views.

Political Rights and Civil Liberties: Citizens of Yemen cannot change their government democratically. Yemen is a republic headed by a popularly elected president, with a bicameral parliament composed of a 301-seat popularly elected House of Representatives and an 111-member Majlis Al-Shura or Consultative Council appointed by the president. The House of Representatives has legislative authority, and the Majlis Al-Shura serves in an advisory capacity.

Yemen is one of the few countries in the Arab world to organize regular elections on national and local levels, with limited competition among the ruling GPC party; two main opposition parties, Islah and the Yemeni Socialist Party (YSP); and a handful of other parties. On the surface level, Yemen appears to have a relatively open democratic system. In reality, Yemen's politics are monopolized by the ruling party, the GPC, which has increased the number of parliament seats it holds from 145 in 1993 to 237 in the current parliament.

Yemen's government suffers from the absence of any real system of checks and balances of power and any significant limits on the executive's authority. Although local council members are popularly elected—the most recent local election was held in 2001—President Ali Abdullah Saleh appoints all local council chairpersons, who wield most of the decision-making authority.

Corruption is an endemic problem at all levels of government and society. Despite recent efforts by the government to step up efforts to fight corruption and institute a civil service reform program, Yemen lacks most legal safeguards to protect against conflicts of interest. Chief auditing and investigative bodies charged with fighting corruption are not sufficiently independent of the executive authorities.

Article 103 of the Press and Publications Law outlaws direct personal criticism of the head of state and publication of material that "might spread a spirit of dissent and division among the people" or "leads to the spread of ideas contrary to the principles of the Yemeni Revolution, [is] prejudicial to national unity or [distorts] the image of the Yemeni, Arab, or Islamic heritage." Although newspapers have some degree of freedom, the print media do not seem to have a strong impact across much of society, which has a high rate of illiteracy, estimated at 54 percent. The state maintains a monopoly over the media that matter the most—television and radio. Access to the Internet is not widespread, and the government reportedly blocks Web sites it deems offensive.

Article 2 of the constitution states that Islam is the religion of state, and Article 3 declares Sharia (Islamic law) to be the source of all legislation. Yemen has few religious minority groups, and their rights are generally respected in practice. Strong politicization of campus life, including tensions between the ruling GPC and opposition Islah parties, places limits on academic freedom.

Yemenis have the right to form associations, according to Article 58 of the constitution. Yemen has several thousand nongovernmental organizations, although some observers question the viability and independence these organizations. The government respects the right to form and join trade unions, but some critics claim that the government and ruling party elements have stepped up efforts to control the affairs of these organizations.

The judiciary is nominally independent, but in practice it is weak and susceptible to interference from the executive branch. Government authorities have a spotty record of enforcing judicial rulings, particularly those issued against prominent tribal or political leaders. The lack of a truly independent judiciary impedes progress in all aspects of democracy and good governance; without an independent arbiter for disputes, people often resort to tribal forms of justice or direct appeals to the executive branch of government.

Arbitrary detention occurs, sometimes because of a lack of proper training of law enforcement officials, and at other times because of a lack of political will at the most senior levels of government. One prominent example of the latter from 2003 was the arrest inside the presidential building and detention without charge of members of the Jahm tribe. The Jahm tribal leaders reportedly had a dispute with officials while in the presidential office, and they were subsequently detained, initially in a military prison. They were ultimately released after mediation from another tribal leader, not because of any procedure related to the courts or the rule of law.

Yemen is relatively homogenous ethnically and racially. The Akhdam, a small minority group, lives in poverty and faces social discrimination.

Women are afforded most legal protections against discrimination and provided with guarantees of equality. In practice, women continue to face pervasive discrimination in several aspects of life. Women are vastly under-represented in elected office. Despite the best efforts of women's rights groups to increase the number of women in parliament, only one woman won a seat in the 2003 parliamentary elections, out of 301 total seats. At the local government level, women won only 38 seats out of 6,676 in the 2001 local elections. The number of women registered to vote increased nearly sevenfold in the past decade, from half a million in the 1993 parliamentary elections to more than three million in the 2003 parliamentary elections.

A woman who seeks to travel abroad must obtain permission from her husband or father to receive a passport and travel. A woman does not have the right to confer citizenship on her foreign-born spouses, and the process of obtaining Yemeni citizenship for a child of a Yemeni mother and a foreign-born father is in practice more difficult than that for a child born of a Yemeni father and a foreign-born mother.

Freedom in the World Methodology

The preceding reports were excerpted from the 2004 edition of *Freedom in the World*, an annual Freedom House survey that monitors the progress and decline of freedom as experienced by individuals in 192 countries and 18 select territories. Freedom is the opportunity to act spontaneously in a variety of fields outside the control of the government and other centers of potential domination. Freedom House measures freedom according to two broad categories: political rights and civil liberties. Political rights enable people to participate freely in the political process, including through the right to vote, compete for public office, and elect representatives who have a decisive impact on public policies and are accountable to the electorate. Civil liberties allow for the freedoms of expression and belief, associational and organizational rights, rule of law, and personal autonomy without interference from the state.

The survey rates each country and territory by assigning points based on questions in a political rights checklist and a civil liberties checklist. The total number of points awarded to each checklist determines the political rights and civil liberties ratings, with 1 representing the highest and 7 the lowest level of freedom [see Tables 1 and 2]. Finally, each country and territory is assigned a broad category status of Free (for countries whose ratings average 1.0 to 2.5), Partly Free (3.0 to 5.0), or Not Free (5.5 to 7.0) [see Table 3]. For a more detailed analysis of the survey methodology, please consult the methodology chapter from *Freedom in the World 2004*.

A change in a country's or territory's political rights or civil liberties rating from the previous year is indicated by an asterisk next to the rating in question, along with a brief ratings change explanation preceding the country or territory report. Freedom House also assigned upward or downward "trend arrows" to certain countries and territories which saw modest positive or negative trends during the year that were not significant enough to warrant a ratings change. Trend arrows are indicated with arrows placed before the name of the country or territory in question, along with a brief trend arrow explanation preceding the report.

The *Freedom in the World* ratings are not only assessments of the conduct of governments, but are intended to reflect the reality of daily life. Freedom can be affected by state actions as well as by non-state actors. Thus, terrorist movements or armed groups use violent methods that can dramatically restrict essential freedoms within a society. Conversely, the existence of non-state activists or journalists who act courageously and independently despite state restrictions can also positively impact the ability of the population to exercise its freedoms.

The survey enables an examination of trends in freedom over time and on a comparative basis across regions with different political and economic systems. The survey, which is produced by a team of in-house regional experts, consultant writers, and academic advisors, derives its information from a wide range of sources. Most valued of these are the many human rights activists, journalists, editors, and political figures around the world who keep us informed of the human rights situation in their countries. *Freedom in the World's* ratings and narrative reports are used by policy makers, leading scholars, the media, and international organizations in monitoring the ebb and flow of freedom worldwide.

POLITICAL RIGHTS AND CIVIL LIBERTIES CHECKLIST
POLITICAL RIGHTS
A. Electoral Process

1. Is the head of state and/or head of government or other chief authority elected through free and fair elections?

2. Are the legislative representatives elected through free and fair elections?

3. Are there fair electoral laws, equal campaigning opportunities, fair polling, and honest tabulation of ballots?

B. Political Pluralism and Participation

1. Do the people have the right to organize in different political parties or other competitive political groupings of their choice, and is the system open to the rise and fall of these competing parties or groupings?

2. Is there a significant opposition vote, de facto opposition power, and a realistic possibility for the opposition to increase its support or gain power through elections?

3. Are the people's political choices free from domination by the military, foreign powers, totalitarian parties, religious hierarchies, economic oligarchies, or any other powerful group?

4. Do cultural, ethnic, religious, and other minority groups have reasonable self-determination, self-government, autonomy, or participation through informal consensus in the decision-making process?

C. Functioning of Government

1. Do freely elected representatives determine the policies of the government?

2. Is the government free from pervasive corruption?

3. Is the government accountable to the electorate between elections, and does it operate with openness and transparency?

Additional discretionary Political Rights questions:

A. For traditional monarchies that have no parties or electoral process, does the system provide for consultation with the people, encourage discussion of policy, and allow the right to petition the ruler?

B. Is the government or occupying power deliberately changing the ethnic composition of a country or territory so as to destroy a culture or tip the political balance in favor of another group?

NOTE: For each political rights and civil liberties checklist question, 0 to 4 points are **added**, depending on the comparative rights and liberties present (0 represents the least, 4 represents the most). However, for additional discretionary question B only, 1 to 4 points are **subtracted**, when necessary.

CIVIL LIBERTIES
D. Freedom of Expression and Belief

1. Are there free and independent media and other forms of cultural expression?
(Note: in cases where the media are state-controlled but offer pluralistic points of view, the survey gives the system credit.)

2. Are there free religious institutions, and is there free private and public religious expression?

3. Is there academic freedom, and is the educational system free of extensive political indoctrination?

4. Is there open and free private discussion?

E. Associational and Organizational Rights

1. Is there freedom of assembly, demonstration, and open public discussion?

2. Is there freedom of political or quasi-political organization? (Note: this includes political parties, civic organizations, ad hoc issue groups, etc.)

3. Are there free trade unions and peasant organizations or equivalents, and is there effective collective bargaining? Are there free professional and other private organizations?

F. Rule of Law

1. Is there an independent judiciary?

2. Does the rule of law prevail in civil and criminal matters? Are police under direct civilian control?

3. Is there protection from police terror, unjustified imprisonment, exile, or torture, whether by groups that support or oppose the system? Is there freedom from war and insurgencies?

4. Is the population treated equally under the law?

G. Personal Autonomy and Individual Rights

1. Is there personal autonomy? Does the state control travel, choice of residence, or choice of employment? Is there freedom from indoctrination and excessive dependency on the state?

2. Do citizens have the right to own property and establish private busi-

nesses? Is private business activity unduly influenced by government officials, the security forces, or organized crime?

3. Are there personal social freedoms, including gender equality, choice of marriage partners, and size of family?

4. Is there equality of opportunity and the absence of economic exploitation?

KEY TO RAW POINTS, POLITICAL RIGHTS AND CIVIL LIBERTIES RATINGS, AND STATUS

Table 4		Table 5	
Political Rights (PR)		**Civil Liberties (CL)**	
Total Raw Points	**PR Rating**	**Total Raw Points**	**CL Rating**
36-40	1	53-60	1
30-35	2	44-52	2
24-29	3	35-43	3
18-23	4	26-34	4
12-17	5	17-25	5
6-11	6	8-16	6
0-5	7	0-7	7

Table 6	
Combined Average of PR and CL Ratings	**Country Status**
1.0 to 2.5	Free
3.0 to 5.0	Partly Free
5.5 to 7.0	Not Free

About Freedom House

Founded in 1941 by Eleanor Roosevelt and others, Freedom House is the oldest non-profit, non-governmental organization in the United States dedicated to promoting and defending democracy and freedom worldwide. Freedom House supports the global expansion of freedom through its advocacy activities, monitoring and in-depth research on the state of freedom, and direct support of democratic reformers throughout the world.

Advocating Democracy and Human Rights: For over six decades, Freedom House has played an important role in identifying the key challenges to the global expansion of democracy, human rights and freedom. Freedom House is committed to advocating a vigorous U.S. engagement in international affairs that promotes human rights and freedom around the world.

Monitoring Freedom: Despite significant recent gains for freedom, hundreds of millions of people around the world continue to endure dictatorship, repression, and the denial of basic rights. To shed light on the obstacles to liberty, Freedom House issues studies, surveys, and reports on the condition of global freedom. Our research is meant to illuminate the nature of democracy, identify its adversaries, and point the way for policies that strengthen and expand democratic freedoms. Freedom House projects are designed to support the framework of rights and freedoms guaranteed in the Universal Declaration of Human Rights.

Supporting Democratic Change: The attainment of freedom ultimately depends on the actions of courageous men and women who are committed to the transformation of their societies. But history has repeatedly demonstrated that outside support can play a critical role in the struggle for democratic rights. Freedom House is actively engaged in these struggles, both in countries where dictatorship holds sway and in those societies that are in transition from autocracy to democracy. Freedom House functions as a catalyst for freedom by working to strengthen civil society, promote open government, defend human rights, enhance justice, and facilitate the free flow of information and ideas.